The Ministry of Intercessory Prayer

Andrew Murray

The Ministry of Intercessory Prayer

BETHANY HOUSE PUBLISHERS
Minneapolis, Minnesota 55438
A Division of Bethany Fellowship, Inc.

Originally published in 1897 under the title, *The Ministry of Intercession*

Edited edition, 1981

Published by Bethany House Publishers
A Division of Bethany Fellowship, Inc.
6820 Auto Club Road, Minneapolis, Minnesota 55438

Printed in the United States of America

Library of Congress Cataloging in Publication Data

Murray, Andrew, 1828-1917.
    The ministry of intercessory prayer.

    Previously published in 1897 as: The ministry of intercession.
    1. Prayer.   I. Title.
BV210.M83   1981   248.3'2   81-18011
ISBN 0-87123-353-3 (pbk.)   AACR2

to
My brethren in the ministry
and
other laborers in the Gospel
whom I was privileged to meet
in the convention at
Langlaagte, Johannesburg, Heilbronn,
Durban, Pietermaritzburg,
King William's Town, Port Elizabeth
and Stellenbosch,
this volume
is affectionately inscribed

ANDREW MURRAY was born in South Africa in 1828. After receiving his education in Scotland and Holland, he returned to that land and spent many years there as both pastor and missionary. He was a staunch advocate of biblical Christianity. He is best known for his many devotional books.

Contents

Books by Andrew Murray

ANDREW MURRAY CHRISTIAN MATURITY LIBRARY

The Believer's Absolute Surrender
The Believer's Call to Commitment
The Believer's Full Blessing of Pentecost
The Believer's New Covenant
The Believer's New Life
The Believer's Secret of a Perfect Heart
The Believer's Secret of Holiness
The Believer's Secret of Living Like Christ
The Believer's Secret of Obedience
The Believer's Secret of the Master's Indwelling
The Spirit of Christ

ANDREW MURRAY PRAYER LIBRARY

The Believer's Prayer Life
The Believer's School of Prayer
The Ministry of Intercessory Prayer
The Secret of Believing Prayer

ANDREW MURRAY DEVOTIONAL LIBRARY

The Believer's Daily Renewal
The Believer's Secret of Waiting on God
Day by Day with Andrew Murray

How to Raise Your Children for Christ
Jesus Christ: Prophet-Priest
Money

There are noble Christian workers,
    The men of faith and power,
The overcoming wrestlers
    Of many a midnight hour;
Prevailing princes with their God,
    Who will not be denied,
Who bring down showers of blessing
    To swell the rising tide.
The Prince of Darkness quaileth
    At their triumphant way,
Their fervent prayer availeth
    To sap his subtle sway.

from "The Ministry of
Intercession" by F. R. Havergal

Introduction

A friend who heard of this book being published asked what the difference would be between it and the previous one on the same subject, *With Christ in the School of Prayer*. An answer to that question may be the best introduction I can give to the present volume.

Any acceptance the former work has had must be attributed, as far as the contents go, to the prominence given to two great truths. The one was, the certainty that prayer will be answered. Some people have an idea that to ask and expect an answer is not the highest form of prayer. They argue that fellowship with God, apart from any request, is greater than supplication. The petition contains something of selfishness and bargaining—to worship is more than to beg.

With others the idea that prayer is often unanswered dominates. They think more of the spiritual benefit derived from the exercise of prayer than the actual gifts to be obtained by it.

I admit the measure of truth in these views. However, *With Christ in the School of Prayer* points out how our Lord continually spoke of prayer as a means of obtaining what we desire, and how He seeks in every possible way to awaken in us the confident expectation of an answer. I was led to show how prayer, in which man enters into the mind of God, asserts the royal power of a renewed will. It brings down to earth that which without prayer would not have been given. It is the highest proof of his being made in the likeness of God's Son.

Man is found worthy of entering into fellowship with God, not only in adoration and worship but in his will actually being instrumental in the rule of the world. In this manner he becomes the intelligent channel through which God can fulfill His eternal purpose. The book sought to reiterate and enforce the precious truth Christ preaches so continually: The blessing of prayer is that you can ask and receive what you will. The highest exercise and the glory of prayer is that persevering importunity can prevail and obtain what God at first could not and would not give.

A second truth became very apparent as we studied the Master's words. Many people question, "But if the answer to prayer is so positively promised, why are there so many unanswered prayers?" We found that Christ taught us that the answer depended upon certain conditions. He spoke of faith, of perseverance, of praying in His name, of praying in the will of God. But all these conditions were summed up in this: "*If ye abide in me* . . . ye shall ask what ye will, and it shall be done unto you" (John 15:7).

It became clear that the power to pray the effectual prayer of faith depended upon *the life in Christ.* A man must give himself up to live as entirely in Christ and for Christ as the branch in the vine and for the vine. Then these promises can come true. "*At that day,*" Christ said of the day of Pentecost, "ye shall ask in my name." Only a life full of the Holy Spirit can know the true power to ask in Christ's name. This led to emphasizing the truth that the ordinary Christian life cannot appropriate these promises. It needs a sound and vigorous spiritual life to pray in power. This teaching naturally led to emphasizing the need of a life of entire consecration. Several have told me how in reading that book they first saw what a better life could be lived—and must be lived—if Christ's wonderful promises are to come true to us.

In regard to these two truths there is no change in the present volume. One only wishes that they could be put with such clarity and force as to help every beloved fellow Christian to comprehend correctly the reality and the glory of our privilege as God's children:"Ask what ye will, and it shall be done unto you."

This book owes its existence to the desire to enforce two truths, of which formerly I had no such understanding. The one is that *Christ meant prayer to be the great power by which His Church should do its work, and that the neglect of prayer is the great reason the Church lacks greater power over the masses in Christian and in heathen countries.* In the first chapter I have stated how my convictions about this have been strengthened, and what inspired the writing of the book. It is meant to be, on behalf of myself and all God's people, a confession of shortcoming and of sin. At the same time it is a call to believe that things can be different, and that Christ waits to enable us by His Spirit to pray as He wants us to pray.

This call brings me back to what I said in connection with the former book: that there is a life in the Spirit, a life of abiding in Christ, within our reach. In that life the power of prayer can be realized in a measure which we could not have thought possible before—both the power to pray and the power to obtain the answer. Any failure in the prayer life, any desire or hope to obtain the place Christ has prepared for us, brings us to the very root of the doctrine of grace as manifested in the Christian life. Only by a full surrender to the life of abiding, by yielding to the fullness of the Spirit's leading and quickening, can the prayer life be restored to a truly healthy state. I feel deeply how inadequately I have been able to express this. I pray and trust that God, who chooses the weak things, will use this book for His own glory.

The second truth which I have tried to emphasize is that *we have far too little understanding of the place that intercession* (as distinguished from prayer for ourselves) *ought to have in the Church and the Christian life.*

Our King upon the throne finds His highest glory in intercession; we shall find our highest glory in it too. Through it He continues His saving work, and can do nothing without it; through it alone we can do our work, and nothing avails without it. In it He continually receives from the Father the Holy Spirit and all spiritual blessings to impart; in it we too are called to receive in ourselves the fullness of God's Spirit, with the power to impart spiritual blessing to others. The power of the Church to bless rests on intercession—*asking and receiving heavenly gifts to carry to men.* When, due to lack of teaching or spiritual insight, we trust in our own diligence and effort to influence the world and the flesh, and work more than we pray, the presence and power of God are not seen in our work as we would wish.

Such thoughts have led me to wonder how to arouse believers to a sense of their high calling in this, and how to help and train them to take part in it. And so this book differs from the former one in the attempt to open a practicing school, and to invite all who have never taken systematic part in the great work of intercession to begin and give themselves to it.

There are tens of thousands of workers who have known and are proving wonderfully what prayer can do. But there are tens of thousands who work with but little prayer and as many more who do not work because they do not know how or where. I desire to persuade them all to join the host of intercessors who are to bring down the blessings of heaven to earth. For their sakes, and for others who need help, I have prepared helps and hints for a school of intercession for a month (see p. 120).

I have asked those who would join to begin by giving at least ten minutes a day to this work. By doing we learn to do. As we take hold and begin, God's Spirit will help. As we daily hear God's call, and at once put it into practice, the consciousness will awaken in us, *I too am an intercessor.* We also shall feel the need of living in Christ and being full of the Spirit in order to do this work in the right way. Nothing will so test and stimulate the Christian life as the honest attempt to be an intercessor.

It is difficult to conceive how much we ourselves and the Church will gain if with our whole heart we accept the position of honor God offers us. I am confident that the first month's course in the school of intercession will awaken us to how little we know how to intercede. A second and a third month may only deepen the sense of ignorance and unfitness. This will be an unspeakable blessing. The confession, "We know not what we should pray for as we ought," is the prerequisite to the experience, "The Spirit . . . maketh intercession for the saints." Our sense of ignorance will lead us to depend upon the Spirit praying in us and to feel the need of living in the Spirit.

We have heard a great deal about systematic Bible study, and we praise God for thousands upon thousands of Bible classes and Bible readings. Let all the leaders of such classes see if they can open *prayer* classes—helping their students to pray in secret, and training them to be men of prayer above all else. Let ministers ask what they can do in this.

Faith in God's Word can nowhere be so exercised and perfected as in the intercession that asks and expects and looks for the answer. Throughout Scripture, in the life of every saint, of God's own Son, throughout the history of God's Church, God is, first of all, a prayer-hearing God. Let us try to help God's children to know their God, and encourage all God's servants to labor with this assurance: *The chief and most blessed part of my work is to ask and receive from my Father what I can bring to others.*

Now you see that what this book contains is the confirmation and the call to put into practice the two great lessons of the former one. "Ask what ye will, and it shall be done unto you"; *"At that day ye shall ask in my name."* These great prayer conditions are universal and unchangeable. A life abiding in Christ and filled with the Spirit, a life entirely given up as a branch for the work of the vine, has the power to claim these promises and to pray the "effectual prayer that availeth much." Lord, teach us to pray.

Andrew Murray
September 1, 1897

CHAPTER ONE

The Lack of Prayer

"Ye have not, because ye ask not" (James 4:2).
"And he saw that there was no man, and wondered that there was no intercessor" (Isa. 59:16).
"There is none that calleth upon thy name, that stirreth up himself to take hold of thee" (Isa. 64:7).

At our last Wellington Convention for the Deepening of the Spiritual Life, the morning meetings were devoted to prayer and intercession. Great blessing was found, both in listening to what the Word teaches of their need and power, and in joining in united supplication. Many felt that we know too little of persevering importunate prayer, and that it is indeed one of the greatest needs of the Church.

During the past two months I attended a number of conventions. At the first, a Dutch Missionary Conference at Langlaagte, prayer was the subject of the messages. At the next, at Johannesburg, a businessman said it was his deep conviction that more of the spirit and practice of intercession was what the Church of our day greatly needed. A week later at a Dutch Ministerial Conference, we spent two days on the work of the Holy Spirit and afterward three days on the relation of the Spirit to prayer. We were led to take up the subject of prayer at the ministers' meetings in succeeding conventions. Everywhere people confessed, "We pray too little!" Along with this there seemed to be a fear that, because of pressure from work and the force of habit, it was almost impossible to hope for any great change.

A deep impression was made upon me by these conversations. There was such hopelessness on the part of God's servants as to the possibility of a complete change being made and real deliverance found, from a failure which cannot but hinder our own joy in God and our power in His service. I prayed God to give me words to direct attention to the evil, but, even more, to stir up faith and inspire assurance that God by His Spirit *will enable us to pray as we ought.*

Let me show some examples that prove how universal is the lack of an adequate prayer life.

Last year in a message to ministers, Dr. Whyte, of Free St. George's, Edinburgh, said that, as a young minister, he had thought that any time left over from pastoral visitation he ought to spend as much as possible in his study with his books. He wanted to feed his people with the very best he could prepare for them. But now he had learned that *prayer* was more important than *study.* He reminded his brethren of the election of deacons to take charge of the collections that the twelve might "give [them]selves continually to prayer and to the ministry of the word." He said that at times, when the deacons brought him his salary, he had to ask himself whether he had been as faithful in his obligations as the deacons had been in theirs. He felt as if it were almost too late to regain what he had lost, and urged his brethren to pray more. What a solemn confession and warning from one of the high places. We pray too little!

During the Regent Square Convention two years ago, the subject arose in conversation with a well-known London minister. He insisted that if so much time must be given to prayer, it would involve the neglect of the imperative calls of duty. The minister said, "There is the morning mail, before breakfast, with ten or twelve letters which *must* be answered. Then there are committee meetings waiting, with countless other engagements, more than enough to fill up the day. It is difficult to see how it can be done."

I answered that it was simply a question of whether the call of God for our time and attention was more important than that of man. If God was waiting to meet us and to give us blessing and power from heaven for His work, it was a short-sighted policy to put other work in the place which God and waiting on Him should have.

At one of our ministerial meetings, the superintendent of a large district stated it this way: "I rise in the morning and have half an hour with God, in the Word and prayer, in my room before breakfast. I go out, and am occupied all day with numerous engagements. I do not think many minutes elapse without my breathing a prayer for guidance or help. After my day's work, I have my evening devotions and speak to God of the day's work. But of the intense, definite, importunate prayer of which Scripture speaks, one knows little." What, he asked, must I think of such a life?

We all see the contrast between a man whose income barely maintains his family and keeps up his business, and a man whose income enables him to expand his business and also help others. There may be an earnest Christian life which has just enough prayer to maintain the position we have attained to, but without much growth in spirituality or Christ-likeness. That is more of a defensive attitude, seeking to fight off temptation, rather than an aggressive one which reaches out after higher attainment. If there is indeed to be a going from strength to strength, and a significant experience of God's power to sanctify ourselves and to bring down real blessing on others, there must be more definite and persevering prayer. The Scripture teaching about crying day and night, continuing steadfastly in prayer, watching unto prayer, being heard for one's importunity, must in some degree become our experience if we are to be intercessors.

The same question was put in somewhat different form at the next convention. "I am at the head of a station, with a large outlying district to care for. I see the importance of much prayer, and yet my life hardly allows time for it. Are we to submit? Or tell us how we can attain to what we desire?"

I admitted that the difficulty was universal.

One of our most honored South African missionaries had the same complaint. "At five in the morning people are at the door waiting for medicine. At six the printers come and I have to set them to work and teach them. At nine the school calls me and till late at night I am kept busy with many letters to answer."

In my answer I quoted a Dutch proverb: " 'What *is* heaviest must *weigh* heaviest'—must have the first place. The law of God is unchangeable; as on earth, so in our communication with heaven, we only get as we give. Unless we are willing to pay the price, to sacrifice time and attention and seemingly legitimate or necessary tasks for the sake of the heavenly gifts, we need not look for much power from heaven in our work."

The whole group united in the sad confession. It had been thought over; it had been mourned over, times without number. Still, there they were, all these pressing claims and all the failures of the resolves to pray more barring the way. Where our conversation led will be found later in this book.

Let me call just one more witness. During my trip I met one of the Cowley Fathers, who held retreats for clergy of the English Church. I was interested to hear the line of teaching he followed. In the course of conversation, he used the expression, "the distraction of business," which he said was one of the great difficulties he had to deal with in himself and others. By the vows of his Order he was bound to give himself especially to prayer. But he found it very difficult. Every day he had to be at four different points of the town he lived in; his predecessor had left him the responsibility of several committees where he was expected to do all the work. It seemed everything conspired to keep him from prayer.

Surely this testimony proves that prayer does not have the place it should have in our ministerial and Christian life. The shortcoming is one which all willingly confess. These examples also reveal that the difficulties blocking deliverance make a return to a true and full prayer life almost impossible.

But . . . blessed be God, "The things which are impossible with men are possible with God"! "God is able to make all grace abound toward you; that ye, always having all sufficiency in all things, may abound to every good work."

God's call to much prayer need not be a burden nor a cause of continual self-condemnation. He means it to be a joy. He can make it an inspiration. Through it He can give us strength for all our work and bring down His power to work through us in our fellowmen.

Without fear let us confess the sin that shames us, and then confront it in the name of our Mighty Redeemer. *The same light that shows us our sin and condemns us for it will show us the way out of it, into the life of liberty that pleases God.* Let this unfaithfulness in prayer convict us of the lack in our Christian life which lies at the root of it. Then God will use the discovery to bring us not only the power to pray that we long for, but also the joy of a new and healthy life, of which prayer is the spontaneous expression.

How can our lack of prayer be transformed into a blessing? How can it be changed into the entrance path where evil may be conquered? How can our relationship with the Father become what it ought to be, one of continual prayer and intercession, so that we and the world around us can be blessed?

We must begin by going back to God's Word to study what place God means prayer to have in the life of His child and His Church. A fresh understanding of what prayer is *according to the will of God,* of what our prayers can be *through the grace of God,* will free us from our weak and impaired attitudes concerning the absolute necessity of continual prayer, which lie at the root of our failure.

As we get an insight into how reasonable and right this divine appointment is, and as we are fully convinced of how wonderfully it fits in with God's love and our own happiness, we shall be freed from the false impression of it being an arbitrary demand. With our whole heart and soul we shall agree and yield to it and rejoice in it as the one and only possible way for the blessing of heaven to come to earth. All thought of task and burden, of self-effort and strain, will pass away. As simple as breathing is in the healthy physical life, so will praying be in the Christian life that is led and filled by the Spirit of God.

As we think about this teaching of God's Word on prayer and accept it, we shall see how our failure in the prayer life results from our failure in the Spirit life. Prayer is one of the most heavenly and spiritual functions of the Spirit life. How could we try or expect to fulfill it so as to please God without our soul being in perfect health and our life possessed and moved by God's Spirit?

The insight into the place God means prayer to take in a full Christian life will show us that we have not been living the true and abundant life. Any thought of praying more, of praying effectively, will be in vain unless we are brought into closer intimacy with our blessed Lord Jesus. Christ is our life. He lives in us in such reality that His life of prayer on earth and of intercession in heaven is breathed into us in the measure that our surrender and our faith allow and accept.

Jesus Christ is the healer of all diseases, the conqueror of all enemies, the deliverer from all sin. Our failure teaches us to turn afresh to Him, to find in Him the grace He gives to pray as we ought. The very humiliation of our past failure may be transformed into our greatest blessing. Pray to God that He will visit our souls and fit us for that work of intercession, which is the greatest need of the Church and the world. Only by intercession can that power be brought down from heaven which will enable the Church to conquer the world.

Stir up the slumbering gift that is lying unused. Seek to gather and train and band together as many as we can, to be God's reminders. Give Him no rest till He makes His Church a joy in the earth. Nothing but intense believing prayer can meet the intense spirit of worldliness complained of everywhere.

CHAPTER TWO

The Ministration of the Spirit and Prayer

"If ye then, being evil, know how to give good gifts unto your children how much more shall your heavenly Father give the Holy Spirit to them that ask him?" (Luke 11:13).

Christ had just said (11:9), "Ask, and it shall be given"; God's giving is inseparably connected with our asking. He applies this principle especially to the Holy Spirit. As surely as a father on earth gives bread to his child, so God gives the Holy Spirit to them that ask Him. The whole ministration of the Spirit is ruled by the one great law: *God must give, we must ask.* When the Holy Spirit was poured out at Pentecost with a flow that never ceases, it was in answer to prayer. His inflow into the believer's heart and His outflow in rivers of living water always depend upon the law, "Ask, and it shall be given."

Along with our confession of the lack of prayer, we also need a clear understanding of the place prayer occupies in God's plan of redemption. Nowhere is this clearer than in the first half of the Acts of the Apostles. The outpouring of the Holy Spirit at the birth of the Church and the first freshness of its heavenly life in the power of that Spirit will teach us how *prayer on earth,* whether as cause or effect, *is the true measure of the presence of the Spirit of heaven.*

We begin with the well-known words, "These all continued with one accord in prayer and supplication." And then there follows, "And when the day of Pentecost was fully come, they were all with one accord in one place. . . . And they were all filled with the Holy Ghost." "And the same day there were added unto them about three thousand souls" (Acts 1:13; 2:1; 2:41).

The great work of redemption had been accomplished. The Holy Spirit had been promised by Christ "not many days

23

hence." He had sat down on His throne and received the Spirit from the Father. But all this was not enough. One thing more was needed: the ten days' united continued supplication of the disciples.

Intense, continued prayer prepared the disciples' hearts, opened the windows of heaven, and brought down the promised gift. The power of the Spirit could not be given without Christ sitting on the throne, nor could it descend without the disciples on the footstool of the throne.

Here at the birth of the Church, the law is laid down for all ages that no matter what else may be found on earth, the power of the Spirit must be prayed down from heaven. The measure of continued believing prayer will be the measure of the Spirit's working in the Church.

Direct, definite, determined prayer is what we need. This is confirmed in Acts, chapter four. Peter and John had been brought before the Council and threatened with punishment. When they returned to their brethren and reported what had been said to them, "they lifted up their voice to God with one accord," and prayed for boldness to speak the Word. "And when they had prayed, the place was shaken . . . and they spake the word of God with boldness. And the multitude of them that believed were of one heart and of one soul. . . . And with great power gave the apostles witness of the resurrection of the Lord Jesus; and great grace was upon them all."

It is as if the story of Pentecost is repeated a second time over, with the prayer, the shaking of the house, the filling with the Spirit, the speaking God's Word with boldness and power, the great grace upon all, the manifestation of unity and love, in order to imprint permanently on the heart of the Church, *it is prayer that lies at the root of the spiritual life and power of the Church.* The degree with which God gives His Spirit is determined by our asking. He gives as a father to him who asks as a child.

In the sixth chapter we find that when people complained about the neglect of the Grecian Jews in the distribution of alms, the apostles proposed the appointment of deacons to serve the tables. "We," they said, "will give ourselves continually to prayer, and to the ministry of the word." It is often and rightly said that there is nothing in honest business (kept in its place as entirely subordinate to the kingdom, which must ever be first) that need prevent fellowship with God. Least of all should ministering to the poor hinder the spiritual life. And yet the apostles felt it would hinder their giving themselves to the ministry of prayer and the Word.

What does this teach? The maintenance of the spirit of prayer is possible in many kinds of work, but it is not enough for those who are the leaders of the Church. To communicate with the King on the throne and keep the heavenly world in clear and fresh focus; to draw down the power and blessing of that world not only for the maintenance of our own spiritual life, but also for those around us; to receive continual instruction and empowerment for the great work to be done—the apostles, as ministers of the Word, felt the need to be free from other duties that they might give themselves to much prayer.

James writes, "Pure religion and undefiled before God and the Father is this, To visit the fatherless and widows in their affliction." If ever any work were a sacred one, it was that of caring for these Grecian widows. Still, even such duties might interfere with the special call to give themselves to prayer and the ministry of the Word. On earth, as in heaven, there is power in the division of labor. Some, like the deacons, had primarily to serve tables and minister the alms of the Church here on earth. Others had to be freed for that steadfast continuance in prayer which would secure the constant downflow of power from the heavenly world.

The minister of Christ is set apart to give himself as much to prayer as the ministry of the Word. Faithful obedience to this law is the secret of the Church's power and success. Before, just as after Pentecost, the apostles were men given up to prayer.

In chapter eight of Acts we have the intimate connection between the Pentecostal gift and prayer from another point of view. At Samaria, Philip had preached with great blessing, and many had believed. But the Holy Spirit had not yet fallen on any of them. The apostles sent down Peter and John to pray for them that they might receive the Holy Spirit.

The power for such prayer was a higher gift than preaching. It was the work of men who had been in closest contact with the Lord in glory. It was a work that was essential to the perfection of the life that preaching and baptism, faith and conversion had only begun. Of all the gifts of the early Church for which we should long there is none more needed than the gift of prayer— prayer that brings down the Holy Spirit on believers. This power is given to the men who say, "We will give ourselves to prayer."

The outpouring of the Holy Spirit, in the house of Cornelius at Caesarea, provides another testimony to the wonderful inter- dependence of prayer and the Spirit. Here is another proof of what will come to a man who has given himself to prayer.

Peter went up at midday to pray on the housetop. What hap- pened? He saw heaven opened, and there came the vision that revealed to him the cleansing of the Gentiles. Then came the message of the three men from Cornelius, a man who "prayed al- way," and had heard from an angel, "Thy prayers are come up before God." Then the voice of the Spirit was heard saying, "Go with them."

It is praying Peter to whom the will of God is revealed, to whom guidance is given as to going to Caesarea, and who is brought into contact with a praying and prepared company of hearers. No wonder that in answer to all this prayer, blessing beyond all expectation comes, and the Holy Spirit is poured out upon the Gentiles.

A minister who is much in prayer will receive an entrance into God's will of which he would otherwise know nothing. He will be brought to praying people where he does not expect them. He will receive blessing above all he asks or thinks. The teaching and the power of the Holy Spirit are unalterably linked to prayer.

The power that the Church's prayer has with its glorified King is shown, not only as the apostles pray but also as the Christian community does. In chapter twelve of Acts we have the story of Peter in prison on the eve of execution. The death of James had aroused the Church to a sense of great danger; the thought of losing Peter, too, wakened up all its energies. It went to prayer. "Prayer was made without ceasing of the church unto God for him."

That prayer was effective. Peter was delivered. When he came to the house of Mary, he found "many were gathered to- gether praying." Stone walls and double chains, soldiers and keepers and then the iron gate—all gave way before the power from heaven that prayer brought down to his rescue.The whole power of the Roman Empire, as represented by Herod, was impotent in the presence of the power that the Church of the Holy Spirit wielded in prayer.

Those Christians stood in close and living relationship with their Lord in heaven. They knew so well that the words "All power is given unto me" and "Lo, I am with you alway" were absolutely true. They had faith in His promise to hear them whatever they asked. Undergirded by these things, they prayed in the assurance that the powers of heaven not only could work on earth, but that they would work at the Church's request and on its behalf. The Pentecostal Church believed in prayer and practiced it.

For one more illustration of the place and the blessing of prayer among men filled with the Holy Spirit, chapter thirteen of Acts names five men at Antioch who had dedicated themselves to ministering to the Lord with prayer and fasting. Their praying was not in vain because as they ministered to the Lord, the Holy Spirit met them and gave them new insight into God's plans. He called them to be fellow workers with himself. There was a work to which He had called Barnabas and Saul. The five men's part and privilege would be to separate Barnabus and Saul with renewed fasting and prayer and to let them go, "sent forth by the Holy Ghost."

God in heaven would not send forth His chosen servants without the co-operation of His Church. Men on earth were to have a partnership in the work of God. Prayer fitted and prepared them for this. To praying men, the Holy Spirit gave authority to do His work and use His name. It was through prayer the Holy Spirit was given. Prayer is still the only secret of true Church extension, prayer that is guided from heaven to find and send forth God-called and God-empowered men.

In answer to prayer, the Holy Spirit will show the men He has selected; in response to prayer that sets them apart under His guidance, He will give the honor of knowing that they are men "sent forth by the Holy Ghost." Prayer links the King on the throne with the Church at His footstool. The Church, the human link, receives its divine strength from the power of the Holy Spirit who comes in answer to prayer.

In these chapters on the history of the Pentecostal Church, how sharply two great truths stand out: *Where there is much prayer, there will be much of the Spirit; where there is much of the Spirit, there will be ever-increasing prayer.* So clear is the living connection between the two that when the Spirit is given in answer to prayer, it stimulates more prayer to prepare for a fuller revelation and communication of His divine power and grace. If prayer was the power by which the primitive Church flourished and triumphed, is it not the one need of the Church of our days?

Let us learn what ought to be counted axioms in our Church work:

1. Heaven is still as full of stores of spiritual blessing as it was then.

2. God still delights to give the Holy Spirit to them that ask Him.

3. Our life and work are still as dependent on the direct impartation of divine power as they were in Pentecostal times.

4. Prayer is still the appointed means for drawing down these heavenly blessings in power on ourselves and those around us.

5. God still seeks for men and women who will, with all their other work of ministering, specially give themselves to persevering prayer.

We may have the privilege of offering ourselves to God to labor in prayer and bring down these blessings to this earth. Shall we not beseech God to make all this truth live in us? Shall we not implore that we not rest until it has mastered us and our whole heart be so filled with it that we count the practice of intercession as our highest privilege? Shall we not ask that we do this which is the sure and only means of obtaining blessing for ourselves, for the Church, and for the world?

CHAPTER THREE

A Model of Intercession

"And he said unto them, Which of you shall have a friend, and shall go unto him at midnight, and shall say unto him, Friend, lend me three loaves; for a friend of mine in his journey is come to me, and I have nothing to set before him? And he from within shall answer and say, Trouble me not: . . . I cannot rise and give thee. I say unto you, Though he will not rise and give him, because he is his friend, yet because of his importunity he will rise and give him as many as he needeth" (Luke 11:5-8).

"I have set watchmen upon thy walls, O Jerusalem, which shall never hold their peace day nor night: ye that [are the Lord's remembrancers] keep not silence. And give him no rest" (Isa. 62:6, 7).

We have now seen what power prayer has. It is the one power on earth that commands the power of heaven. The story of the early days of the Church is God's great object lesson to teach His Church what prayer can do. Prayer alone can pull down the treasures and powers of heaven into the life of earth.

Remember the lessons we learned of how prayer is at once indispensable and irresistible. We saw that unknown and untold power and blessing is stored up for us in heaven; that power will make us a blessing to men, and fit us to do any work or face any danger; that it is to be sought in prayer continually and persistently; that they who have the heavenly power can pray it down upon others; that in all the relationships between ministers and people, in all the ministrations of Christ's Church, it is the one secret of success; that it can defy all the power of the world, and fit men to conquer that world for Christ. The power of the heavenly life, the power of God's own Spirit, the power of Omnipotence, waits for prayer to bring it down.

In all this type of prayer there was little thought of personal need or happiness. Rather, there was desire to witness for Christ and bring Him and His salvation to others. It was the thought of

God's kingdom and glory that possessed these disciples. If we would be delivered from the sin of restraining prayer, we must enlarge our hearts for the work in intercession.

The attempt to pray constantly for ourselves must be a failure. It is in intercession for others that our faith and love and perseverance will be aroused and that power of the Spirit be found which can fit us for saving men. How may we become more faithful and successful in prayer? Let us see in the parable of the Friend at Midnight (Luke 11) how the Master teaches us that intercession for the needy calls forth the highest exercise of our power of believing and prevailing prayer. Intercession is the most perfect form of prayer; it is the prayer Christ ever lives to pray on His throne. Let us learn what the elements of true intercession are.

1. *Urgent need.* Here intercession has its origin. The friend came at midnight, an untimely hour. He was hungry and could not buy bread. If we are to learn to pray as we should, we must open eye and heart to the need around us.

We hear continually of the billions of heathen and Muslims living in midnight darkness, perishing for lack of the bread of life. We hear of millions of nominal Christians, the great majority of them almost as ignorant and indifferent as the heathen. We see millions in the Christian Church, not ignorant or indifferent, and yet knowing little of a walk in the light of God or of the power of a life fed by bread from heaven. Each of us has his own circle—congregation, school, friends, mission—in which the great complaint is that the light and life of God are too little known. But if we believe what we profess, that God alone is able to help, that God certainly will help in answer to prayer, all this ought to make intercessors of us. It should motivate us to be people who give their lives to prayer for those around them.

Let us face and consider the need—each Christless soul going down into outer darkness, perishing of hunger, while there is bread enough and to spare! Millions each year die without the knowledge of Christ! Our own neighbors and friends, souls entrusted to us, die without hope! Christians around us live sickly, feeble, fruitless lives! Surely prayer is needed. Nothing—nothing but prayer to God for help will avail.

2. *Willing love.* The friend took his weary, hungry friend into

his house and into his heart too. He did not excuse himself by saying he had no bread. At midnight he went out to seek it for him. He sacrificed his night's rest and his comfort to find the needed bread. Love "seeketh not her own." It is the very nature of love to give up and forget itself for the sake of others. It takes their needs and makes them its own. It finds its real joy in living and dying for others as Christ did.

The love of a mother for her prodigal son makes her pray for him. True love for souls will become in us the spirit of intercession. It is possible to do much faithful and earnest work for our fellowmen without true love for them. Just as a lawyer or a physician, from a love of his profession and a high sense of faithfulness to duty, may become deeply involved with the needs of clients or patients without any special love for them, so servants of Christ may give themselves to their work with devotion and self-sacrificing enthusiasm without any strong, Christlike love for souls. It is this lack of love that causes so much shortcoming in prayer. Only as love of our profession and work, delight in thoroughness and diligence, sink away in the tender compassion of Christ, that love will compel us to prayer, because we cannot rest in our work if souls are not saved. True love must pray.

3. *The sense of impotence.* We often speak of the power of love. In one sense this is true, and yet the truth has its limitations, which must not be forgotten. The strongest love may be utterly impotent. A mother might be willing to give her life for her dying child but still not be able to save it. The friend at midnight was most willing to give his friend bread, but he had none. It was this sense of impotence, of his inability to help, that sent him begging, "A friend . . . is come to me, and *I have nothing* to set before him." This sense of impotence in God's servants is the very strength to the life of intercession.

"I have nothing to set before him." As this consciousness possesses the minister or missionary, the teacher or worker, intercession becomes the only hope and refuge. I may have knowledge and truth, a loving heart, and the readiness to give myself for those under my charge, but the bread of heaven I cannot give them. With all my love and zeal "I have nothing to set before them."

Blessed the man who has made the declaration "I have nothing" the motto of his ministry. He thinks of the judgment day and the danger of souls. He sees what a supernatural power and life is needed to save men from sin. He feels how utterly insufficient he is—all he can do is to meet their natural need. *"I have nothing"* urges him to pray. As he thinks of the midnight darkness and the hungry souls, intercession appears to him as the only hope, the one thing in which his love can take refuge.

As a warning to all who are strong and wise to work, for the encouragement of all who are feeble, remember this truth. The sense of impotence is the soul of intercession. The simplest, feeblest Christian can pray down blessing from an Almighty God.

4. *Faith in prayer.* What the man himself has not, another can supply. He has a rich friend nearby who will be both able and willing to give the bread. He is sure that if he only asks, he will receive. This faith makes him leave his home at midnight; if he himself has not the bread to give, he can ask another.

We need this simple, confident faith that God will give. Where it really exists, there will surely be no possibility of our not praying. In God's Word we have everything that can arouse and strengthen such faith in us. The heaven our natural eye sees is one great ocean of sunshine, with its light and heat giving beauty and fruitfulness to earth. In the same manner, Scripture shows us God's true heaven, which is filled with all spiritual blessings—divine light and love and life, heavenly joy and peace and power, all shining down upon us. It reveals to us our God waiting, even delighting, to bestow these blessings in answer to prayer.

By a thousand promises and testimonies, Scripture calls and urges us to believe that prayer will be heard, that what we cannot possibly do ourselves for those whom we want to help can be done and received by prayer. Surely there can be no question as to our believing that prayer will be heard. We see also that through prayer the poorest and feeblest can dispense blessings to the needy, and each of us, even though poor, may yet be making many rich.

5. *Importunity that prevails.* The faith of the friend met a sudden and unexpected obstacle—the rich friend refuses to hear. "I cannot rise and give thee." The loving heart had not counted on this disappointment. It cannot consent to accept it. The supplicant presses his threefold plea: Here is my needy friend; you

have abundance, I am your friend. Then he refuses to accept a denial. The love that opened his house at midnight and then left it to seek help must conquer.

Here is the central lesson of the parable. In our intercession we may find that there is difficulty and delay in the answer. It may be as if God says, "I cannot give thee." It is not easy, against all appearances, to hold fast our confidence that He will hear, and then to continue to persevere in full assurance that we shall have what we ask. Even so, this is what God desires from us. He highly prizes our confidence in Him, which is essentially the highest honor the creature can render the Creator. He will therefore do anything to train us in the exercise of this trust in Him. Blessed the man who is not staggered by God's delay or silence or apparent refusal, but is strong in faith giving glory to God. Such faith perseveres, importunately, if need be, and cannot fail to inherit the blessing.

6. *Certainty of a rich reward.* "I say unto you . . . because of his importunity he will rise and give him as many as he needeth." Oh, that we might believe in the certainty of an abundant answer! A prophet said of old: "Let not your hands be weak; *for your work shall be rewarded.*" Would that all who feel it difficult to pray much would fix their eye on the reward, and in faith learn to count upon the divine assurance that their prayer cannot be in vain.

If we will only believe in God and His faithfulness, intercession will become to us the very first thing we take refuge in when we seek blessing for others. It will be the very last thing for which we cannot find time. Also it will become a thing of joy and hope, because all the time we pray, we recognize that we are sowing seed that will bring forth fruit an hundredfold. Disappointment is impossible: "I say unto you . . . he will rise and give him as many as he needeth."

Lovers of souls and workers in the service of the gospel, take courage. Time spent in prayer will yield more than that given to work. Prayer alone gives work its worth and its success. Prayer opens the way for God himself to do His work in us and through us. Let our chief work as God's messengers be intercession; in it we secure the presence and power of God to go with us.

"Which of you shall have a friend . . . at midnight, and say unto him, Friend, lend me three loaves?" This friend is none other than our God. In the darkness of midnight, at the most unlikely time and in the greatest need, when we have to say of those we love and care for, "I have nothing to set before them," let us remember that we have a rich Friend in heaven. The Everlasting God and Father only waits to be asked aright.

Let us confess before God our lack of prayer. Let us admit that the lack of faith, of which lack of prayer is the proof, is the symptom of a life that is not spiritual, that is yet under the power of self and the flesh and the world. Let us by faith in the Lord Jesus, who spoke this parable and waits to make every trait of it true in us, give ourselves to be intercessors. Let every sight of souls needing help, let every stirring of the spirit of compassion, let every sense of our own impotence to bless, let every difficulty in the way of our getting an answer, all combine only to urge us to do this one thing: with importunity to cry to the God who alone can and will help.

But if we indeed feel that we have failed in a life of intercession until now, let us do our utmost to train a young generation of Christians, who profit by our mistake and avoid it. Moses could not enter the land of Canaan, but there was one thing he could do. He could at God's bidding "charge Joshua, and encourage him, and strengthen him" (Deut. 3:28). If it is too late for us to make good our failure, let us at least encourage those who come after us to enter into the good land, the blessed life of unceasing prayer.

The model intercessor is the model Christian worker. To get from God, and then to give to men what we ourselves secure from day to day, is the secret of successful work. Intercession is the blessed link between our impotence and God's omnipotence.

CHAPTER FOUR

Because of His Importunity

"I say unto you, Though he will not rise and give him, because he is his friend, yet *because of his importunity* he will rise and give him as many as he needeth" (Luke 11:8).

"And he spake a parable unto them to this end, that men ought always to pray, and not to faint. . . . Hear what the just judge saith. And shall not God avenge his own elect, which *cry day and night unto him, though he bear long with them*? I tell you that he will avenge them speedily" (Luke 18:1:6-8).

Our Lord Jesus thought it so important for us to know the need of perseverance and importunity in prayer that He gave two parables to teach us this. This is sufficient proof that this aspect of prayer contains prayer's greatest difficulty and its highest power. He would have us know that in prayer all will not be so easy and smooth. We must expect difficulties, which can be conquered only by persistent, determined perseverance.

In the parables our Lord represents the difficulty as existing on the side of the persons to whom the petition was addressed, that importunity is needed to overcome their reluctance to hear. Between God and us, however, the difficulty is not on His side, but on *ours*. In the first parable He tells us that our Father is more willing to give good things to those who ask Him than any earthly father is to give his child bread. In the second, He assures us that God longs to avenge His elect speedily.

Urgent prayer is not needed because God must be made willing or disposed to bless. The need lies altogether in ourselves. However, it was not possible to find any earthly illustration of a loving father or a willing friend from whom the needed lesson of importunity could be taught. He therefore uses the unwilling friend and the unjust judge to encourage in us the faith that perseverance can overcome every obstacle.

35

The difficulty is not in God's love or power, but in ourselves and our own incapacity to receive the blessing. But because there is this difficulty with us, this lack of spiritual preparedness, there is a difficulty with God too. His wisdom, His righteousness, even His love, dare not give us what would do us harm if we received it too soon or too easily.

The sin, or the consequence of sin, that makes it impossible for God to give at once is a barrier on God's side as well as ours. The attempt to break through this power of sin in ourselves or those for whom we pray is what makes the striving and the conflict of prayer such a reality.

Throughout history men have prayed under a sense that there were difficulties in the heavenly world to overcome. They pleaded with God for the removal of the unknown obstacles. In that persevering supplication they were brought into a state of utter brokenness and helplessness, of entire resignation to Him, of union with His will, and of faith that could take hold of Him. Then the hindrances in themselves and in heaven were together overcome. *As God conquered them, they conquered God.* As God prevails over us, we prevail with God.

God has so constituted us that the more clearly we see the reasonableness of a demand, the more heartily we will surrender to it. One great cause of our negligence of prayer is that there appears to be something arbitrary or at least something incomprehensible in the call to such continued prayer. We need to see that this apparent difficulty is a divine necessity and that in the very nature of things it is the source of unspeakable blessing. Then we should be ready with gladness of heart to give ourselves to continue in prayer. Let us try to understand how the call to importunity and the difficulty that it throws in our way is one of our greatest privileges.

Have you ever noticed what a part difficulties play in our natural life? They call forth man's power as nothing else can. They strengthen and ennoble character. We are told that one reason for the superiority of the northern nations (e.g., Holland and Scotland) in strength of will and purpose over those of the sunny South, such as Italy and Spain, is that the climate of the latter has been too mild; the life it encourages is too easy and relaxing.

The difficulties the northern nations have to contend with have been their greatest boon.

All nature has been so arranged by God that in sowing and reaping, just as in seeking coal or gold, nothing is found without labor and effort. What is education but a daily developing and disciplining of the mind by new difficulties which the pupil must overcome? The moment a lesson has become easy, the pupil is advanced to one that is higher and more difficult. Collectively and individually, it is in confronting and mastering difficulties that our highest attainments are found.

It is even so in our relationship with God. Imagine what the result would be if the child of God had only to kneel down, ask, get, and go away. What unspeakable loss to the spiritual life would result. In the very difficulty and delay that calls for persevering prayer will the true blessing and blessedness of the heavenly life be found. There we learn how little we delight in fellowship with God and how little we have of living faith in Him. We discover how earthly and unspiritual our heart still is, how little we have of God's Holy Spirit. There we are brought to know our own weakness and unworthiness and to yield to God's Spirit to pray in us. There we take our place in Christ Jesus and abide in Him as our only plea with the Father. There our own will and strength and goodness are crucified. There we rise in Christ to newness of life because now our whole will is dependent on God and set upon His glory. Let us begin to praise God for the need and the difficulty of importunate prayer as one of His choicest means of grace.

Just think what our Lord Jesus owed to the difficulties in His path. In Gethsemane it was as if the Father would not hear. He prayed yet more earnestly until "he was heard." In the way He opened up for us, He learned obedience by the things He suffered and thus was made perfect. His will was given up to God. His faith in God was proved and strengthened. The prince of this world with all his temptation was overcome. This is the new, the living way He consecrated for us. It is in persevering prayer that we walk with and are made partakers of His very Spirit. Prayer is one form of crucifixion, of our fellowship with Christ's cross, of our giving up our flesh to the death.

Oh, Christians, shall we not be ashamed of our reluctance to sacrifice the flesh, our own will and the world, as we so clearly show in our reluctance to pray much? Shall we not learn the lesson which nature and Christ alike teach? The difficulty of importunate prayer is our highest privilege. The difficulties to be overcome in it bring us our richest blessings.

Importunity has various elements. The chief ones are perseverance, determination, and intensity. Importunity begins with the refusal to readily accept a denial. This refusal develops into a determination to persevere, to spare no time or trouble, until an answer comes. Then this determination grows into an intensity in which the whole being is given to God in supplication. Boldness comes to lay hold of God's strength. At one time it is quiet and restful; at another, passionate and bold. At one point it waits in patience, but at another, it claims at once what it desires. In whatever different shape, importunity always means and knows, *God hears prayer; I must be heard.*

Remember the wonderful examples we have of importunity in the Old Testament saints. Think of Abraham as he pleads for Sodom. Time after time he renews his prayer until the sixth time he has to say, "Let not the Lord be angry." He does not cease until he has learned to know God's condescension in each time consenting to his petition, until he has learned how far he can go, has entered into God's mind, and has rested in God's will. For his sake Lot was saved. "God remembered Abraham, and sent Lot out of the midst of the overthrow." Shall not we who have a redemption and promises for the heathen which Abraham never knew begin to plead more with God on their behalf?

Think of Jacob when he feared to meet Esau. The angel of the Lord met him in the dark and wrestled with him. When the angel saw that he did not prevail, he said, "Let me go." Jacob said, "I will not let thee go." So the angel blessed him there. That boldness that declared "I will not," and forced from the reluctant angel the blessing, so pleased God that a new name was given to Jacob: Israel, he who strives with God, "for thou hast striven with God and with men, and hast prevailed."

Through all ages God's children have understood what Christ's two parables teach, that God holds himself back and seeks to get away from us until what is of flesh and self and laziness in us is overcome. Then we can prevail with Him so that He *can* and *must* bless us.

Why is it that so many of God's children have no desire for this honor of being princes of God, strivers with God, and prevailing? What our Lord taught us, "What things soever ye desire . . . *believe that ye receive them,*" is nothing but His expression of Jacob's words, "I will not let thee go except thou bless me." This is the importunity He teaches. We must learn—to claim and take the blessing.

Think of Moses when Israel had made the golden calf. Moses returned to the Lord and said, "Oh, this people have sinned a great sin. . . . Yet now, if thou wilt forgive their sin—; and if not, blot me, I pray thee, out of thy book which thou hast written." That was importunity. Moses would rather have died than not have his people given him.

When God had heard him and said He would send His angel with the people, Moses came again. He would not be content until in answer to his prayer God himself should go with them (33:12, 17, 18), God had said, "I will do this thing also that thou hast spoken." After that, in answer to Moses' prayer, "Show me thy glory," God made His goodness pass before him. Then Moses at once began pleading, "Let my Lord, I pray thee, go among us." "And he was there with the Lord forty days and forty nights" (Ex. 34:28).

As an intercessor, Moses used importunity with God, and prevailed. He proves that the man who truly lives near to God, and with whom God speaks face to face, partakes of that same power of intercession which there is in Jesus, who is at God's right hand and ever lives to pray.

Think of Elijah in his prayers, first for fire and then for rain. In the former, his importunity claims and receives an immediate answer. In the latter, he bows himself down to the earth, his face between his knees. His answer to the servant who had gone to look toward the sea and come with the message, "There is nothing," was, "Go again seven times." Here was the importunity of perseverance. Elijah had told Ahab there would be rain. He knew it was coming. Still he prayed until the seven times were fulfilled.

It is of Elijah and this prayer that James teaches, "Pray one for another." "[Elijah] was a man subject to like passions as we are." "The effectual fervent prayer of a righteous man availeth much." Will there not be some who feel constrained to cry out, "Where is the Lord God of Elijah?"—this God who draws forth such effectual prayer, and hears it so wonderfully. His name be praised. He still waits to be inquired of! Faith in a prayer-hearing God will make a prayer-loving Christian.

Remember the marks of the true intercessor as taught in the parable: a sense of the need of souls, a Christlike love in the heart, a consciousness of personal impotence, faith in the power of prayer, courage to persevere in spite of refusal, and the assurance of an abundant reward. These are the qualities that change a Christian into an intercessor and call forth the power of prevailing prayer.

These are the elements that mark the Christian life with beauty and health. They fit a man for being a blessing in the world, and make him a true Christian worker, one who obtains from God the bread of heaven to dispense to the hungry. These are the attitudes that call forth the highest, the heroic virtues of the life of faith.

There is nothing to which the nobility of natural character owes more than the spirit of enterprise and daring which *battles* with difficulties in travel or war, in politics or science, and *conquers*. No labor or expense is grudged for the sake of victory. So should we who are Christians be able to face the difficulties that we meet in prayer. As we "labor" and "strive" in prayer, the renewed will asserts its royal right to claim in the name of Christ what it will, and wield its God-given power in influencing the destinies of men.

Men of the world sacrifice ease and pleasure in their pursuits. Shall we be such cowards and sluggards as not to fight our way through to the place where we can find liberty for the captive and salvation for the perishing? Let each servant of Christ learn to know his calling. His King ever lives in us to pray. The Spirit of the King ever lives in us to pray. It is from heaven that the blessings which the world needs must be called down in persevering, importunate, believing prayer. From heaven the Holy Spirit, in answer to prayer, will take complete possession of us to do His work through us.

Let us acknowledge how vain our much work has been due to our little prayer. Let us change our method and make more prayer, much prayer, unceasing prayer, be the proof that we look to God for all, and that we believe that He hears us.

CHAPTER FIVE

The Life That Can Pray

"If ye abide in me, and my words abide in you, ye shall ask what ye will, and it shall be done unto you" (John 15:7).

"The effectual fervent prayer of *a righteous man* availeth much" (James 5:16).

"Beloved, if our heart condemn us not, then we have confidence toward God. And whatsoever we ask, we receive of him, *because* we keep his commandments, and do those things that are pleasing in his sight" (1 John 3:21, 22).

Here on earth the influence of one who asks a favor for others depends entirely on his character, and the relationship he has to him with whom he is interceding. *It is what he is that gives weight to what he asks.* It is no different with God. Our power in prayer depends upon our life. When our life is right, we shall know how to pray so as to please God, and prayer will secure the answer.

The texts quoted above all point in this direction. "If ye abide in me," our Lord says, "ye shall ask . . . and it shall be done unto you." According to James, it is the prayer of *a righteous man* that "availeth much." We receive "whatsoever we ask," John says, *because* we obey and please God.

All lack of power to pray aright and with perseverance, all lack of power in prayer with God, points to some lack in the Christian life. Only as we learn to live the life that pleases God will God give what we ask.

Let us learn from our Lord Jesus, in the parable of the vine, what the healthy, vigorous life is that may ask and receive what it will. He says, "If ye abide in me, and my words abide in you, ye shall ask what ye will, and it shall be done unto you." He says at the close of the parable, "Ye have not chosen me, but I have chosen you, and ordained you, that ye should go and bring forth fruit, and that your fruit should remain: that *whatsoever ye shall ask* of the Father in my name, *he may give it you."*

What is, according to the parable, the life that one must lead to bear fruit and then ask and receive what we will? What must we be or do that will enable us to pray as we should and to receive what we ask? The answer is in one word: it is the *branch* life that gives power for prayer. We are branches of Christ, the Living Vine. We must simply live like branches and abide in Christ; then we shall ask what we will and it shall be done for us.

We all know what a branch is and what is its essential characteristic. It is simply a growth of the vine, produced by it and appointed to bear fruit. It has only one purpose: it is there at the bidding of the vine, that through it the vine may bear and ripen its precious fruit. Just as the vine soley and wholly lives to produce the sap that makes the grape, so the branch has no other aim and object but to receive that sap and bear the grape. Its only work is to serve the vine that through it the vine may do its work.

Is it to be understood that the believer, the branch of Christ the Heavenly Vine, is just as literally and exclusively to live only so Christ may bear fruit through him? Is it meant that a true Christian as a branch is to be just as absorbed in and devoted to the work of bearing fruit to the glory of God as Christ the Vine was on earth and now is in heaven? This and nothing less is what is meant. It is to such a person that the unlimited prayer promises of the parable are given.

It is the branch-life, existing solely for the Vine, that will have the power to pray aright. With our life abiding in Him, and His words abiding and ruling in our heart and life, transmuted into our very being, there will be the grace to pray aright, and the faith to receive the "whatsoever we will."

Let us connect the two concepts and take them both in their simple, literal truth and their infinite, divine grandeur. The promises of our Lord's farewell discourse, with their wonderful sixfold repetition of the unlimited, *anything, whatsoever* (John 14:13, 14; 15:7, 16; 16:23, 24), appear to us altogether too large to be taken literally. Therefore we rationalize them to meet our human ideas of what it appears they ought to be. We separate them from that life of absolute and unlimited devotion to Christ's service for which they were given.

God's covenant is always, *give all and take all.* He that is willing to be wholly branch and nothing but branch, who is ready to place himself absolutely at the disposal of Jesus the Vine of God, to bear His fruit through him, and to live every moment only for Him, will receive a divine liberty to claim Christ's *whatsoever* in all its fullness and a divine wisdom and humility to use it properly.

Such a person will live and pray and claim the Father's promises, even as Christ did, only for God's glory in the salvation of men. He will use his boldness in prayer only with a view to power in intercession and getting men blessed. The unlimited devotion of the branch life to fruit-bearing and the unlimited access to the treasures of the Vine life are inseparable. It is the life abiding wholly in Christ that can pray the effective prayer in the name of Christ.

Think for a moment of the men of prayer in Scripture, and see in them what the life was that could pray in such power. We spoke of Abraham as intercessor. What gave him such boldness? He knew that God had chosen and called him away from his home and people to walk before Him so that all nations might be blessed in him. He knew that he had obeyed and forsaken all for God. Implicit obedience, to the very sacrifice of his son, was the law of his life. He did what God asked so he dared trust God to do what he asked.

We spoke of Moses as intercessor. He too had forsaken all for God, "esteeming the reproach of Christ greater riches than the treasures of Egypt." He lived at God's disposal, "as a servant he was faithful in all his house." How often it is written of him, "According to all that the Lord commanded Moses, so did he." No wonder that he was very bold. His heart was right with God. He knew God would hear him. No less true is this of Elijah, the man who stood up to plead for the Lord God of Israel. The man who is ready to risk all for God can count upon God to do all for him.

Men pray only as they live. It is the life that prays. The life that with wholehearted devotion gives up all for God and to God can also claim all from God. Our God longs to prove himself the faithful God and mighty helper of His people. He only waits for hearts wholly turned from the world to himself and open to receive His gifts. The man who loses all will find all and will dare ask and take it.

The branch that only and truly abides in Christ, the Heavenly Vine, is entirely given up like Christ to bear fruit in the salvation of men. It has His words taken up into and abiding in its life, and may dare ask what it will—and it shall be done.

Where we have not yet attained to that full devotion to which our Lord had trained His disciples, and cannot equal them in their power of prayer, we may, nevertheless, take courage in one fact. Even in the lower stages of the Christian life, every new onward step in the striving after the perfect branch life, and every surrender to live for others in intercession, will be met from above by a corresponding liberty to draw nigh with greater boldness and expect larger answers. The more we pray and the more conscious we become of our inability to pray in power, the more we shall be urged and helped to press on toward the secret of power in prayer—a life abiding in Christ, entirely at His disposal.

If any are asking with despair of attainment what the reason may be for failure in this blessed branch life, so simple and yet so mighty, and are asking how they can attain it, let me point them to one of the most precious lessons of the parable of the Vine. It is one that is neglected. Jesus said, "I am the true Vine, *and my Father is the husbandman.*" We have not only Jesus himself, the glorified Son of God, in His divine fullness and out of whose fullness of life and grace we can draw—this is wonderful—but there is something even more blessed. We have the Father, as the husbandman, watching over our abiding in the Vine, over our growth and fruit-bearing. It is not left to our faith or our faithfulness to maintain our union with Christ. God, the Father of Christ and who united us with Him—God himself—will see to it that the branch is what it should be. He will enable us to bring forth just the fruit we were appointed to bear. Hear what Christ said of this, "Every branch that beareth fruit, he cleanseth it, that it may bear more fruit." More fruit is what the Father seeks; more fruit is what the Father himself will provide. It is for this that He, as the Vinedresser, prunes the branches.

Consider what this means. It is said that of all fruit-bearing plants on earth, there is none that produces fruit so full of spirit and from which spirit can be so abundantly distilled as the vine.

And of all fruit-bearing plants there is none that is so ready to produce wild wood and for which pruning is so indispensable. The one great work that a vinedresser has to do for the branch every year is to prune it. Other plants can for a time dispense with it and still bear fruit; the vine *must* have it. So the branch that desires to abide in Christ and bring forth much fruit and to be able to ask whatsoever it will, must do one thing: trust in and yield itself to this divine cleansing.

What does the vinedresser cut away with his pruning knife? He cuts the wood that the branch has produced—true, honest wood with the true vine nature in it.

Why must this be cut away? Because it draws away the strength and life of the vine and hinders the flow of the juice to the grape. The more it is cut down, the less wood there is in the branch and the more all the sap can go to the grape. The wood of the branch must decrease that the fruit for the vine may increase. In obedience to the law of all nature, that death is the way to life, that gain comes through sacrifice, the rich and luxuriant growth of wood must be cut off and cast away that the more abundant life may be seen in the cluster.

In the same way, child of God, branch of the Heavenly Vine, there is in you that which appears perfectly innocent and legitimate but which saps away your interest and strength. It must be pruned and cleansed. We saw what power in prayer men like Abraham, Moses, and Elijah had, and we know what fruit they bore. But we also know what it cost them. God had to separate them from their surroundings over and over to draw them from any trust in themselves, so they would seek their life in Him alone.

It is only as our own will, our strength, our effort, our pleasure, are cut down—even where these appear perfectly natural and sinless—that the whole energies of our being are free and open to receive the sap of the Heavenly Vine, the Holy Spirit. Then we shall bear much fruit. It is in the surrender of what nature holds fast in the full and willing submission to God's holy pruning knife that we shall come to what Christ chose and appointed us for—to bear fruit, that whatsoever we ask the Father in Christ's name, He may give to us.

Christ tells us what the pruning knife is in the next verse: "Ye

are *clean through the word* which I have spoken unto you." As He
says later, "Sanctify them through thy truth; thy word is truth."
"The word of God is . . . sharper than any two-edged sword,
piercing even to the dividing . . . of soul and spirit."

Christ had spoken to His disciples heart-searching words on
love and humility, on being the least, and, like himself the servant of all, on denying self, and taking the cross, and losing the
life. Through His word, the Father had cleansed them, cut away
all confidence in themselves or the world and prepared them for
the inflowing and filling of the Spirit of the Heavenly Vine. We
cannot cleanse ourselves. God is the Vinedresser. We may confidently entrust ourselves to His care.

Beloved brethren—ministers, missionaries, teachers, workers, believers old and young—are you mourning your lack of
prayer and the resultant lack of power in prayer? Then come and
listen to your beloved Lord as He tells you, "Only be a branch.
Unite to and identify with the Heavenly Vine, and your prayers
will be effective and avail much."

Are you mourning because that is your exact trouble—you do
not, *cannot,* live this branch-life, abiding in Him? Come and listen again. *"More fruit"* is not only your desire but the Father's
too. He is the Husbandman who cleanses the fruitful branch that
it may bear more fruit.

Cast yourself upon God to do in you what is impossible to
man. Count upon a divine cleansing to cut down and take away
all that self-confidence and self-effort that has been the cause of
your failure. The God who gave you His beloved Son to be your
Vine, who made you His branch, will He not do His work of
cleansing to make you fruitful in every good work, in the work of
prayer and intercession too?

Here is the life that can pray: A branch entirely given up to
the Vine and its aims with all responsibility for its cleansing cast
on the Vinedresser, a branch that is abiding in Christ and trusting and yielding to God for His cleansing, can bear much fruit. In
the power of such a life we shall love prayer, we shall know how to
pray, we shall pray and receive whatsoever we ask.

CHAPTER SIX

Is Prayerlessness Sin?

"Thou . . . restrainest prayer before God" (Job 15:4).

"What profit should we have, if we pray unto him?" (Job 21:15).

"God forbid that I should sin against the Lord in ceasing to pray for you" (1 Sam. 12:23).

"Neither will I be with you any more, except ye destroy the accursed from among you" (Josh.7:12).

Any deep quickening of the spiritual life of the Church will always be accompanied by a deeper sense of sin. This will not begin with theology, which can only describe what God works in the life of His people. Nor does it mean that that deeper sense of sin will be seen only in stronger expressions of self-reproach or penitence (that sometimes indicates a harboring of sin, and unbelief as to deliverance).

The true sense of the hatefulness of sin and the hatred of it will be proved by the intensity of desire for deliverance, and the struggle to know to the very utmost what God can do in saving from it—a holy jealousy, which desires to sin against God in nothing.

If we are to deal effectively with the lack of prayer, we must look at it from this point of view and ask, "Is prayerlessness sin?" If it is, how can it be dealt with—discovered, confessed, cast out by man and cleansed away by God?

Jesus is a Savior from sin. Only as we know sin truly can we know the power that saves from sin. The life that can pray effectively is the life of the cleansed branch—the life that knows deliverance from the power of self. To see that our prayer-sins are indeed sins is the first step toward a true and divine deliverance from them.

The story of Achan has one of the strongest proofs in Scripture that sin robs God's people of His blessing, and that God will not tolerate it. At the same time it gives the clearest indication of the principles under which God deals with sin and removes it. In the light of the story, let us see if we can learn how to look at the sin of prayerlessness and at the sinfulness that lies at its root. The words, "Neither will I be with you any more, except ye destroy the accursed from among you," take us into the very heart of the story. They suggest a series of priceless lessons around the truth they express, that the presence of sin makes the presence of God impossible.

1. *The presence of God is the great privilege of God's people and their only power against the enemy.* God had promised to Moses, "I will bring you in unto the land." Moses proved that he understood this when God, after the sin of the golden calf, spoke of withdrawing His presence and sending an angel. Moses refused to accept anything less than God's presence. "For wherein shall it be known here that I and thy people have found grace in thy sight? Is it not in that thou goest with us?"

This gave Caleb and Joshua their confidence: the Lord is with us. This gave Israel their victory over Jericho: the presence of God. This is throughout Scripture the great central promise: *I am with thee.* This separates the wholehearted believer from the unbelievers and worldly Christians around him—he lives consciously hidden in the secret of God's presence.

2. *Defeat and failure are always due to the loss of God's presence.* This was true at Ai. God had brought His people into Canaan with the promise to give them the land. When the defeat at Ai took place, Joshua felt at once that the cause must be in the withdrawal of God's power. God had not fought for them. His presence had been withheld.

In the Christian life and the work of the Church, defeat is always a sign of the loss of God's presence. If we apply this to our failure in the prayer life, which leads to failure in our work for God, we then see that all is simply due to our not standing in clear and full fellowship with God. His nearness, His immediate presence, has not been the chief thing sought after and trusted in. He could not work in us as He would. Loss of blessing and power is always caused by the loss of God's presence.

3. *The loss of God's presence is always due to some hidden*

sin. Just as pain is nature's warning of some hidden evil in the system, defeat is God's voice telling us there is something wrong. He has given himself wholly to His people. He delights in being with them and revealing in them His love and power. Therefore, He never withdraws himself unless they compel Him to do so by sin.

Throughout the Church there is a complaint of defeat. The Church has so little power over the masses or the educated classes. Powerful conversions are comparatively rare. The lack of holy, consecrated, spiritual Christians, devoted to the service of God and their fellowmen, is felt everywhere. The power of the Church for the preaching of the gospel to the heathen is paralyzed by the scarcity of money and men. This is due to the lack of the effective prayer which brings the Holy Spirit in power, first on ministers and believers, then on missionaries and the heathen. Can we deny that the lack of prayer is the sin which prevents God's presence and power from being manifested among us?

4. *God himself will reveal the hidden sin.* We may think we know what the sin is but it is only God who can reveal its real deep meaning. When He spoke to Joshua, before naming the sin of Achan, God first said, "They have also transgressed my covenant which I commanded them." God had commanded that all the booty of Jericho, the gold and silver and all that was in it, was to be consecrated unto the Lord, and was to come into His treasury. Israel had broken this consecration vow. It had not given God His due. It had robbed God.

It is this we need: God must reveal to us that lack of prayer is the indication of unfaithfulness to our consecration vow that gave God all our heart and life. We must see that prayerlessness, with the excuses we make for it, is greater sin than we have thought; because, what does it mean? It means that we have little taste or relish for fellowship with God. It shows that our faith rests more on our own work and efforts than on the power of God. It shows we have little sense of the heavenly blessing God waits to shower down. It shows we are not ready to sacrifice the ease and confidence of the flesh for persevering, for waiting on God. It shows that the spirituality of our life and our abiding in Christ is altogether too feeble to make us prevail in prayer.

When the pressure of work for Christ becomes the excuse for our not finding time to seek and secure His own presence and power as our chief need, it proves that there is no right sense of our absolute dependence upon God. There is obviously no deep grasp of the divine and supernatural work of God in which we are only His instruments. There is no true entrance into the heavenly, other-worldly character of our mission and aims, nor is there full surrender to, and delight in, Christ Jesus himself.

If we were to yield to God's Spirit to show us that all this reveals our neglect of prayer, and of our allowing other things to crowd it out, all our excuses would fall away. We would fall down and cry, "We have sinned! we have sinned!" Samuel once said, "As for me, God forbid that I should sin against the Lord in ceasing to pray for you." Ceasing from prayer is sin against God. May God reveal this to us (Appendix 1).

5. *When God discloses sin, it must be confessed and cast out.* When the defeat at Ai came, Joshua and Israel were ignorant of the cause. God dealt with Israel as a nation, as one body, and the sin of one member was visited on all. Israel as a whole was ignorant of the sin but still suffered for it. The Church may be ignorant of the greatness of this sin of prayerlessness. Individual ministers or believers may never have looked upon it as actual transgression. Even so, the punishment which it brings is still sure and certain.

But when the sin is no more hidden, when the Holy Spirit begins to convict, then comes the time of heart-searching. In our story the combination of individual and corporate responsibility is very solemn. In the expression "man for man," each man felt himself under the eye of God, to be dealt with. And when Achan had been taken, he had to make confession. In the corporate aspect, we see all Israel first suffering and being dealt with by God, then taking Achan and his family and the accursed thing, and destroying them out of their midst.

If we have reason to think prayerlessness is the sin that is in our camp, let us begin with personal and united confession. Then let us come before God to put away and destroy the sin. At the very threshold of Israel's history in Canaan this heap of stones stands in the valley of Achor, to tell us that God cannot bear sin, that God will not dwell with sin, and that *if we really want God's presence in power, sin must be put away.*

Let us look the solemn fact in the face. There may be other sins, but here is certainly one that causes the loss of God's presence—not praying as Christ and Scripture teach us. Let us uncover it before God and give up this sin to death. Let us yield ourselves to God to obey His voice. Let no fear of past failure, let no threatening array of temptations or duties or excuses keep us back. It is a simple question of obedience. Are we going to give up ourselves to God and His Spirit to live a life in prayer, well-pleasing to Him?

If it is God who has been withholding His presence, exposing the sin, calling for its destruction and a return to obedience, surely we can count upon His grace to accept and strengthen for the life He asks of us. It is not a question of what you can do. It is a question of whether you now, with your whole heart, will give God His due and allow His will and grace to have their way with you.

6. *When sin is cast out, God's presence is restored.* From this day onwards there is not a word in the book of Joshua of defeat in battle. The story shows the Israelites going on from victory to victory. God's presence gives power to overcome every enemy.

This truth is so simple that the very ease with which we agree to it robs it of its power. Let us pause and think what it implies. God's presence restored means victory secured. Then, if there is defeat, we are responsible for it. Sin somewhere must be causing it. We need at once to discover the sin and put it away. The moment the sin is put away, we may confidently expect God's presence. Surely each person is under the solemn obligation to search his life and see what part he may have in this evil.

God never speaks to His people of sin except with a view to saving them from it. *The same light that shows the sin will show the way out of it.* The same power that breaks down and condemns will, if humbly yielded to and waited on, with confession and faith, give the power to rise up and conquer.

It is God who is speaking to His Church and to us about this sin: "He wondered that there was no intercessor." "I wondered that there was none to uphold." "I sought for a man that should stand in the gap before me, and found none." The God who speaks thus is He who will work the change in His children who seek His face. He will make the valley of Achor—of trouble and shame of sin confessed and cast out—a door of hope.

Let us not fear. Let us not cling to the excuses and explanations which circumstances suggest. But let us simply confess, "We have sinned; we are sinning; we dare not sin any longer."

In this matter of prayer we are sure God does not demand of us impossibilities. He does not weary us with an impracticable ideal. He asks us to pray no more than He gives grace to enable us to do so. He will give the grace to do what He asks, to pray that our intercessions shall, day by day, be a pleasure to Him and to us, a source of strength to our conscience and our work, and a channel of blessing to those for whom we labor.

God dealt personally with Joshua, with Israel, with Achan. We must each allow Him to deal personally with us concerning this sin of prayerlessness, its consequences in our life and work, concerning the deliverance from sin, its certainty and blessedness.

Bow in stillness and wait before God until, as God, He overshadows you with His presence. Wait until He leads you out of that region of argument as to human possibilities, where conviction of sin can never be deep and full deliverance can never come. Be still before God in a time of quiet that He may deal with this matter at hand. "Sit still, for he will not be at rest until he has finished this thing this day." Leave yourself in God's hands.

CHAPTER SEVEN

Who Shall Deliver?

"Is there no balm in Gilead; is there no physician there? why then is not the health of the daughter of my people recovered?" (Jer. 8:22).

"Return, ye backsliding children, and I will heal your backslidings. Behold, we come unto thee; for thou art the Lord our God" (Jer. 3:22).

"Heal me, O Lord, and I shall be healed" (Jer. 17:14).

"O wretched man that I am! who shall deliver me from the body of this death? I thank God through Jesus Christ our Lord. . . . The law of the Spirit of life in Christ Jesus hath made me free from the law of sin and death" (Rom. 7:24; 8:2).

During one of our conventions a gentleman called upon me for advice and help. He was evidently an earnest and well-instructed Christian man. For some years he had been in extremely difficult surroundings, trying to witness for Christ. The result was a sense of failure and unhappiness. His complaint was that he had no desire for the Word nor joy in it, and that though he prayed, it was as if his heart was not in it. If he spoke to others or gave a tract, it was under a sense of duty. Love and joy were not present in the doing of them. He longed to be filled with God's Spirit, but the more he sought it, the farther off it appeared to be. What was he to think of his state? Was there any way out of it?

My answer was that the whole matter appeared to me very simple. He was living under the law and not under grace. As long as he did so, there could be no change. He listened attentively but could not understand what I meant.

I pointed out the complete contrast between law and grace. Law demands. Grace bestows. Law commands but gives no strength to obey. Grace promises and performs, doing all we need to do. Law burdens and casts down and condemns. Grace comforts and makes strong and glad. Law appeals to self to do its utmost. Grace points to Christ to do all. Law calls to effort and strain and urges us toward a goal we never can reach. Grace works in us all God's blessed will.

I explained to the man that, rather than striving against all this failure, he should first acknowledge it fully, and then face the reality of his own impotence as God had been trying to teach him. With this confession of failure and impotence, he should sink down before God in utter helplessness. There he would learn that unless grace gave him deliverance and strength, he never could do better than he had done. But grace would indeed work all that was needed for him. He must come out from under law and self and effort and take his place under grace, allowing God to do all.

Later he told me the diagnosis had been correct. He admitted grace must do all. But still, so deep was the thought that we *must do something*, that we must at least by our faithfulness help to receive the work of grace, that in reality he feared that his life would not be very different. He feared that he would not be equal to the strain of new difficulties into which he was now going. Amid all the intense earnestness, I sensed that an undertone of despair reigned; he was certain he could not live as he knew he ought to.

I had noticed this frequent tone of hopelessness before. Every minister who has come into close contact with souls who are seeking to live wholly for God, to "walk worthy of the Lord unto all well pleasing," knows that this renders true progress impossible. When we speak of lack of prayer, and the desire to live a fuller prayer life, how many are the difficulties we face! We have so often resolved to pray more and better, and have failed.

We have not the strength of will some have, so that with one resolve we turn round and change our habits. The pressure of our daily responsibility is as great as ever it was; it is as difficult as ever to find time for more prayer. We do not feel a real enjoyment in prayer, which would enable us to persevere. We do not possess the power to plead with God in intercession as we know we should. Our prayers, instead of being a joy and a strength, are a source of continual self-condemnation and doubt. We have at times mourned and confessed our prayerlessness and resolved to do better; but we do not expect an answer, for we see no way for any great change to take place.

As long as this spirit prevails, there can be very little hope of improvement. Discouragement brings defeat. One of the first objects of a physician is to awaken hope; without this he knows his medicines will often profit little. No teaching from God's Word as to the duty, the urgent need, the blessed privilege of more, and effective prayer, will avail while the secret whisper is heard: There is no hope.

Our first purpose here is to find out the hidden cause of the failure and despair, and then to give divine assurance of deliverance. Unless we are to rest content with our state, we must listen to and join in the question, "Is there no balm in Gilead; is there no physician there? why then is not the health of the daughter of my people recovered?" We must listen, and receive into our heart, the divine promise, "Return, ye backsliding children, and I will heal your backslidings. Behold, we come unto thee, for thou are the Lord our God."

We must come with the personal prayer, and with faith that there will be a personal answer. We must even now begin to claim it in regard to the lack of prayer, and believe that God will help us: "Heal me, O Lord, and I shall be healed."

It is always important to distinguish between the symptoms of a disease and the disease itself. Feebleness and failure in prayer is a sign of feebleness in the spiritual life. If a patient were to ask a physician to give him something to stimulate his feeble pulse, he would be told that this would do him little good. The pulse is the index of the state of the heart and the whole system. The physician strives to have health restored.

Everyone who wants to pray more faithfully and effectively must learn that his whole spiritual life is in a sickly state, and needs restoration. As he looks, not only at his shortcomings in prayer, but at the lack in the life of faith, of which this is the symptom, he will become fully alive to the serious nature of the disease. He will then see the need of a radical change in his whole life and walk, if his prayer life—which is simply the pulse of the spiritual system—is to indicate health and vigor.

God has so created us that the exercise of every healthy function causes joy. Prayer is meant to be as simple and natural as breathing or working to a healthy man. The reluctance we feel, and the failure we confess, are God's own voice calling us to acknowledge our disease, and to come to Him for the healing He has promised.

What is the disease of which the lack of prayer is the symptom? We cannot find a better answer than is pointed out in the words, "Ye are not under the law, but under grace."

We have suggested here the possibility of two types of Christian life. There may be a life partly under the law and partly under grace; or a life entirely under grace, in the full liberty from self-effort and the full experience of the divine strength which it can give. A true believer may still be living partly under the law, in the power of self-effort, striving to do what he cannot accomplish. The continued failure in his Christian life which he admits is due to this one thing: *He trusts in himself and tries to do his best.* He does, indeed, pray and look to God for help, but still it is he in his strength, helped by God, who is to do the work.

In the Epistles to the Romans, Corinthians, and Galatians, Paul tells believers that they have not received the spirit of bondage again, that they are free from the law, that they are no more servants but sons. He warns them to beware of becoming entangled again with the yoke of bondage. He continually draws the contrast between the law and grace, between the flesh, which is under the law, and the Spirit, who is the gift of grace, and through whom grace does all its work.

In our days, just as in those first ages, the great danger is living under the law, and serving God in the strength of the flesh. With the great majority of Christians it appears to be the state in which they remain all their lives. This explains the tremendous lack of true holy living and power in prayer. They do not know that all failure can have but one cause: *Men seek to do themselves what grace alone can do in them,* what grace most certainly will do.

Many will not be prepared to admit that this is their disease, that they are not living "under grace." Impossible, they say. "From the depth of my heart," a Christian cries, "I believe and know that there is no good in me, and that I owe everything to grace alone." "I have spent my life," a minister says, "and found my glory in preaching and exalting the doctrines of free grace." "And I," a missionary answers, "how could I ever have thought of seeing the heathen saved if my only confidence had not been in the message I brought, and the power I trusted, of God's abounding grace?" Surely you cannot say that our failures in prayer—and we sadly confess to them—are owed to our not living "under grace"? This cannot be our disease.

We know how often a man may be suffering from a disease without knowing it. What he counts a slight ailment turns out to be a dangerous problem. Do not be too sure that we are not still largely living "under the law," while considering ourselves to be living wholly "under grace."

Very frequently the reason for this mistake is the limited meaning attached to the word "grace." Just as we limit God himself by our small or unbelieving thoughts of Him, so we limit His grace at the very moment that we are delighting in terms like the "riches of grace," "grace exceeding abundant." From Bunyan's book downward, has not the very term "grace abounding" been confined to the one great blessed truth of free justification with ever renewed pardon and eternal glory for the vilest of sinners, while the other equally blessed truth of "grace abounding" in sanctification is not fully known?

Paul writes, "Much more they which receive abundance of grace . . . shall reign in life through Jesus Christ." That reigning in life, as conqueror over sin, is even here on earth. "Where sin abounded" in the heart and life, "grace did much more abound . . . even so might grace reign through righteousness" in the whole life and being of the believer. It is about this reign of grace in the soul that Paul asks, "Shall we continue in sin, that grace may abound?" and answers, "God forbid."

Grace is not only pardon of, but *power over,* sin; grace takes the place sin had in the life. Grace undertakes, as sin had reigned within in the power of death, to reign in the power of Christ's life. It is of this grace that Christ spoke, "My grace is sufficient for thee." Paul answered, "[I will] glory in my infirmities . . . for, when I am weak, then am I strong." When we are willing to confess ourselves utterly impotent and helpless, his grace comes in to work all in us, as Paul elsewhere teaches, "God is able to make *all grace* abound toward you; that ye, *always* having *all sufficiency* in *all things,* may abound to *every good work.*"

Often a seeker after God and salvation has read his Bible long, and still has never seen the truth of a free and full and immediate justification by faith. When once his eyes were opened, and he accepted it, he was amazed to find it everywhere. Even many believers, who hold the doctrines of free grace as applied to pardon, have never seen its wondrous meaning. It undertakes to work our whole life in us, and *actually give us strength every moment* for whatever the Father would have us be and do. When God's light shines into our heart with this blessed truth, then we understand Paul's words, "Not I, but the grace of God." There again you have the twofold Christian life. The one, in which that "not I"—I am nothing, I can do nothing—has not yet become a reality. The other, when the wondrous exchange has been made and grace has taken the place of our effort. Then we say and know, "I live; yet not I, but Christ liveth in me." It may then become a lifelong experience. "The grace of our Lord was exceeding abundant with faith and love which is in Christ Jesus."

Do you think it is possible that this has been the lack in your life, the cause of your failure in prayer? You knew not how grace would enable you to pray if once the whole life were under its power. You sought by earnest effort to conquer your reluctance or deadness in prayer, but failed. By shame or love you tried to overcome your failure but they did not help. Is it not worthwhile to ask the Lord whether the message I bring you may not be more true for you than you think?

Your lack of prayer is due to a diseased state of life. The disease is nothing but this—you have not accepted, for daily life and every duty, the full salvation which the word brings: "Ye are not under the law, but under grace." As universal and deep-reaching as the demand of the law and the reign of sin is the provision of grace and the power by which it makes us reign in life (Appendix 2).

Paul wrote, "Ye are not under the law, but under grace," and in the chapter that follows he gives us a picture of a believer's life under law. This life ends with the bitter experience, "O wretched man that I am! who shall deliver me from the body of this death?" His answer, "I thank God through Jesus Christ our Lord," shows that there is deliverance from a life held captive under evil habits that have been struggled against in vain.

Deliverance is by the Holy Spirit giving the full experience of what the life of Christ can work in us; "The law of the Spirit of life in Christ Jesus hath made me free from the law of sin and death." The law of God could only deliver us into the power of the law of sin and death. The grace of God can bring us into, and keep us in, the liberty of the Spirit. We can be made free from the sad life under the power that led us captive, so that we did not what we would. The Spirit of life in Christ can free us from our continual failure in prayer and enable us in this, too, to walk worthy of the Lord unto all well-pleasing.

Do not despair or lose hope, because there is a remedy. There is a Physician. There is healing for our sickness. What is impossible with man is possible with God. What you see no possibility of doing, grace will do. Confess the disease. Trust the Physician. Claim the healing. Pray the prayer of faith, "Heal me, and I shall be healed." You too can become a man of prayer, and pray the effective prayer that avails much.*

---

*I ought to say, for the encouragement of all, that the gentleman of whom I spoke, at a convention two weeks later, saw and claimed the rest of faith in trusting God for all. A letter from England tells that he has found that His grace is sufficient.

CHAPTER EIGHT

Wilt Thou Be Made Whole?

"Jesus . . . saith unto him, Wilt thou be made whole? The impotent man answered him, Sir, I have no man . . . to put me into the pool. Jesus saith unto him, Rise . . . and walk. Immediately the man was made whole . . . and walked" (John 5:6-9).

"Peter said . . . In the name of Jesus Christ of Nazareth rise up and walk. . . . The faith which is by him hath given him this perfect soundness in the presence of you all" (Acts 3:6, 16).

"Peter said, Eneas, Jesus Christ maketh thee whole: arise. . . . And he arose immediately" (Acts 9:34).

Feebleness in prayer is the mark of disease.

In the Christian life just as in the natural life, impotence to walk is a terrible proof of some evil in the system that needs a physician. This lack of power to walk joyfully in the new and living way that leads to the Father and the throne of grace is especially grievous. Christ is the great Physician, who comes to every Bethesda where sickly folk are gathered, and speaks out His loving, searching question, "Wilt thou be made whole?"

For all who are still clinging to their hope in the pool or are looking for some man to put them in, for those who are hoping to be helped somehow in the course of time by just continuing to use ordinary means of grace, His question points out a better way. He offers them healing in a way of power they have never understood. To all who are willing to confess, not only their own impotence, but their failure to find any man to help them, His question brings the sure and certain hope of a forthcoming deliverance.

We have seen that our weakness in prayer is part of a life afflicted with spiritual impotence. Listen to our Lord as He offers to restore our spiritual strength, to fit us for walking like healthy, strong men in all the ways of the Lord, and in that way to be well equipped to take our place in the great work of intercession. As we see what the wholeness is which He offers, how He gives it, and what He asks of us, we shall be prepared to give a willing answer to His question.

The Health That Jesus Offers

There are many marks of spiritual health. Our text leads us to one—*walking*. Jesus said to the sick man, Rise and walk. He restored the man to his place among men in full health and vigor, able to take his part in all the work of life. It is a wonderfully suggestive picture of the restoration of spiritual health. To the healthy, walking is a pleasure; to the sick, it is a burden, if not an impossibility. How many Christians there are to whom, like the maimed and the halt and the lame and the impotent, movement and progress in God's way is indeed an effort and a weariness. Christ comes to tell us, and with the word He gives the power, "Rise and walk."

This walk to which He restores and empowers us—it is a life like that of Enoch and Noah, who "walked with God." It is a life like that of Abraham, to whom God said, "Walk before me," and who himself said, "The Lord before whom I walk." It is a life of which David sings, "They walk . . . in the light of thy countenance," and Isaiah prophesies, "They that wait upon the Lord shall renew their strength; . . . they shall run, and not be weary; and they shall walk, and not faint."

God the Creator does not faint and is not weary, and they who walk with Him and wait on Him shall never be exhausted or feeble. It is a life like the last of the Old Testament saints, Zacharias and Elisabeth of whom it was said, "They were both righteous before God, walking in all the commandments and ordinances of the Lord blameless." This is the walk Jesus came to make possible to His people in greater power than ever before.

The New Testament describes it: "That like as Christ was raised up from the dead by the glory of the Father, even so we also should walk in newness of life." It is the Risen One who says to us, "Rise and walk." He gives the power of the resurrection life. It is a *walk in Christ*. "As ye therefore received Christ Jesus the Lord, so walk ye in him." It is a *walk like Christ*. "He that saith he abideth in him ought himself also so to walk, even as he walked." It is a *walk in the Spirit and after the Spirit.* "Walk in the Spirit, and ye shall not fulfill the lust of the flesh." "Who walk not after the flesh, but after the Spirit." It is a *walk worthy of God and well pleasing to Him.* "That ye might walk worthy of the Lord, unto all pleasing, being fruitful in every good work." "We beseech you . . . that as ye have received of us how ye ought to walk and to please God, so ye would abound more and more." It is a *walk in heavenly love.* "Walk in love, as Christ also hath loved us." It is a *"walk in the light, as he is in the light."* It is a *walk of faith,* all its power coming from God and Christ and the Holy Spirit, to the soul turned away from the world. "We walk by faith, not by sight."

How many believers there are who regard such a walk as an impossible thing—so impossible that they do not feel it a sin that they "walk otherwise." Therefore they do not desire this walk in newness of life. They have become so accustomed to the life of impotence that the life and walk in God's strength has little attraction.

But there are some for whom this is not true. They wonder if these words really mean what they say, if the wonderful life of which those verses speak is simply an unattainable ideal, or if it is meant to be realized in this present life. The more they study these admonitions, the more they feel sure that they are given for daily life. But they still appear too idealistic. How wonderful if they would believe this walk to be possible, to believe that God indeed sent His Almighty Son and His Holy Spirit to call us and prepare us for an earthly life to be lived with heavenly power beyond anything that man could dare to imagine or hope for.

How Jesus Makes Us Whole

When a physician heals a patient, he acts on him from without, and tries to render the patient independent of his doctor's aid. The physician restores the patient to perfect health and then leaves him. The work of our Lord Jesus is in both of these ways the very opposite. Jesus works not from without but from *within.* He enters in the power of His Spirit into our very life.

Christ's purpose in healing is the exact opposite of bodily healing which aims, if possible, toward independence from the

physician. Christ's condition of success is to bring us into *such
dependence upon himself that we shall not be able one single moment to live without Him.*

Christ Jesus himself is our life in a sense that many Christians cannot conceive. The prevailing feeble and sickly Christian
life is entirely due to the lack of the appropriation of divine truth.
As long as we expect Christ continually to do something for us
from heaven, in single acts of grace from time to time, and each
time to trust Him to give us only that which will last a little
while, we cannot be restored to perfect health. But when once we
see how there is to be nothing of our own for a single moment,
that it is to be all Christ moment by moment, and so we learn to
accept it from Him and trust Him for it, then the life of Christ becomes the health of our soul.

Health is nothing but life in its normal, undisturbed activity.
Christ gives us health by giving us himself as our life; so He becomes our strength for our walk. Isaiah's words thus find their
New Testament fulfillment: They that wait on the Lord shall
walk and not faint, because Christ is now the strength of their
life.

It is strange how believers sometimes think this life of dependence is too great a strain; they deplore a loss of personal liberty.
They admit a need of dependence, of much dependence, but with
room left for the exercise of their own will and energy. They do
not see that even a partial dependence makes them debtors, and
leaves them nothing to boast of. They forget that their relationship to God, and cooperation with Him, is not that He does the
larger part and they the lesser, but that God does all and they do
all—God all in me, I all through God.

This dependence upon God secures one's true independence.
When our will seeks nothing but the divine will, we reach a divine
nobility, the true independence of all that is created. He that has
not seen this must remain a sickly Christian, letting self do part
and Christ part. He that accepts the life of unceasing dependence
on Christ as his life and health and strength is made whole.

As God, Christ can enter and become the life of His creature.
As the Glorified One who received the Holy Spirit from the
Father, in order to give it away, Christ can renew the heart of the
sinful creature. He can make it His home, and by His presence

maintain it in full health and strength.

You who desire to walk in a way that pleases God, and not have your heart condemn you in your prayer life, listen to Christ's words: "Wilt thou be made whole?" He can give soul-health. He can give a life that can pray, that is well pleasing to the Father. If you want this, come and hear how you can receive it.

What Christ Asks of Us

The opening text invites us to notice three specific things. Christ's question first appeals to the will, and asks for its *consent*. Then He listens to the man's *confession* of his utter helplessness. Next comes the *response* to Christ's command, the ready obedience that rises up and walks.

First is the question, "Wilt thou be made whole?" Who would not be willing to have his sickness removed? But, it is sad to see that there is need to repeat the question. Some will not admit that they are really sick. Some will not believe that Christ can make a man whole. Some can believe others are sick—but they are sure it is not for them.

At the root of all lies the fear of the self-denial and the sacrifice which will be required. People are not willing to forsake entirely the walk after the course of this world, to give up all self-will, self-confidence, and self-pleasing. The walk in Christ and like Christ is too straight and hard. They do not want it. They do not want to be made whole. If you are willing to be made whole, confess clearly: "Lord, at any price, I will!" From Christ's side the act is also one of the will: "I will, be thou clean." From your side equally: "Be it unto thee as thou wilt." If you would be delivered from your impotence, do not be afraid to say, "I will, I will!"

Then comes the second step. Christ wants you to look to Him as your only helper. "I have no man to put me in" must be your cry. Here on earth there is no help for you. Weakness may grow into strength with normal care if all the organs and functions are in a sound state. Sickness needs special measures. Your soul is sick; your impotence and inability to maintain a joyful Christian walk in God's way is a sign of disease. Do not be afraid to confess it and admit that there is no hope of restoration for you unless an act of Christ's mercy heals you. Give up the idea of growing out of your sickly state into a healthy one, of growing out from under the law into a life under grace.

A few days ago I heard a student defend the cause of the Volunteer Pledge. "The pledge calls you," he said, "to a decision. Do not think of growing into a missionary. Unless God forbids you, take the step. The decision will bring joy and strength, will set you free to develop in every way needed for a missionary, and will be a help to others." It is also like that in the Christian life. Delay and struggle will equally hinder you.

Confess that you cannot bring yourself to pray as you would, because you cannot give yourself the healthy, heavenly life that loves to pray, and that knows how to count upon God's Spirit to pray in us. Come to Christ to heal you. In one moment He can make you whole, not in the sense of working a sudden change in your feelings, or in what you are in yourself, but in heavenly reality He will come, in response to your surrender and faith. He will take charge of your inner life, and fill it with himself and His Spirit.

The third thing Christ asks is the surrender of faith. When He spoke to the impotent man, His command had to be obeyed. The man believed that there was truth and power in Christ's word; in that faith he rose and walked. By faith he obeyed. What Christ said to others was for him too—"Go thy way; thy faith hath made thee whole." Of us, too, Christ asks this faith. His word changes our impotence into strength, and equips us for that walk in newness of life for which we have been invigorated by Him.

If we do not believe this, if we will not muster the courage to say with Paul, "I can do all things through Christ which strengtheneth me," we cannot obey. But if we will listen to the word that tells us of the walk that is not only possible, but has been proved and seen in God's saints from of old, if we will fix our eye on the mighty, living, loving Christ, who speaks in power, "Rise and walk," we shall take courage and obey. We shall rise and begin to walk in Him and His strength. In faith—apart from and above all feeling—we shall accept and trust an unseen Christ as our strength, and go on in the strength of the Lord God. We shall know Christ as the strength of our life. We shall know, and tell, and prove that Jesus Christ has made us whole.

Can it be? Yes, it can. He has done it for many; He will do it for you. Beware of forming wrong conceptions of what must take place. When the impotent man was made whole, he still had to learn everything about how to use his new-found strength. If he wanted to dig, or build, or learn a trade, he had to start at the beginning. Do not expect at once to be proficient in prayer or any part of the Christian life. But expect and be confident that, as you have trusted yourself to Christ to be your health and strength, He will lead and teach you. Begin to pray in a quiet sense of your ignorance and weakness, but in a joyful assurance that He will work in you what you need. Rise and walk each day in a holy confidence that He is with you and in you. Accept Jesus Christ the Living One, and trust Him to do His work.

Will you do it? Have you done it? Even now Jesus speaks, "Rise and walk." Reply, "Amen, Lord, at your word I come. I rise to walk with you, and in you, and like you."

CHAPTER NINE

The Secret of Effective Prayer

"What things soever ye desire, when ye pray, believe that ye receive them, and ye shall have them" (Mark 11:24).

Here we have a summary of our Lord Jesus' teaching on prayer. Nothing will so greatly help to convince us of the sin of our lack of prayer, to reveal its causes, and to give us courage to expect entire deliverance, as the careful study and then the believing acceptance of that teaching.

The more heartily we enter into the mind of our blessed Lord, and set ourselves to think about prayer as He thought, the more surely will His words be as living seeds. They will grow and produce in us their fruit—a life and practice exactly corresponding to the divine truth they contain. Let us believe this: Christ, the living Word of God, gives in His words a divine quickening power which brings into being what they say. It works in us what He asks, and actually fits and enables for all He demands. Learn to view His teaching on prayer as a definite promise of what He, by His Holy Spirit dwelling in you, is going to work into your very being and character.

Our Lord gives us the five marks, or essential elements, of true prayer. First, there must be the heart's *desire*; then the expression of that desire in *prayer*; with that, the *faith* that carries the prayer to God; in that faith, the *acceptance of God's answer*; then comes *the experience* of the desired blessing. It may help to clarify our thought if we each take a definite request about which to learn to pray in faith. Better still, we should all unite in the one thing that has been occupying our attention. After speaking of failure in prayer, why should we not take as the object of desire and intercession the "grace of supplication"? We each can say, "I

68

want to ask and receive in faith the power to pray just in the way and just as much as my God expects of me." Let us meditate on our Lord's words in the confidence that He will teach us how to pray for this blessing.

1. "What things soever *ye desire*." Desire is the secret power that moves the whole world of living men, and directs the course of each. Desire is the soul of prayer, and the cause of insufficient or unsuccessful prayer is often found in the lack or weakness of desire. Some may doubt this; they are sure that they have very earnestly desired what they ask. But if they judge whether their desire has indeed been as wholehearted as God would have it, as much as the heavenly worth of these blessings demands, they may come to see that it was indeed the lack of desire that was the cause of failure.

What is true of God is true of each of His blessings, and is the more true the more spiritual the blessing: "Ye shall seek me, and find me, when ye shall search for me with all your heart" (Jer. 29:13). It is written of Judah in the days of Asa, "[They] sought him with their whole desire" (2 Chron. 15:15).

A Christian may often have very strong desires for spiritual blessings. But alongside of these there are other desires in his daily life occupying a large place in his interests and affections. The spiritual desires are not all-absorbing. He is puzzled that his prayer is not heard. It is simply because God wants the whole heart. "The Lord our God is one Lord; and thou shalt love the Lord thy God with all thine heart." The law is unchangeable; God offers himself, gives himself away, to the wholehearted who wholly give themselves away to Him. He always gives us according to our heart's desire, not as we think of our desire but as He sees it. If there are other desires which are more at home with us, which occupy more of our heart than He himself and His presence, He allows these to be fulfilled, and the desires that we are asking for at the hour of prayer cannot be granted.

We desire the gift of intercession, grace and power to pray aright. Our hearts must be drawn away from other desires; we must give ourselves wholly to this one. We must be willing to live wholly in intercession for the kingdom. By fixing our eye on the blessedness and the need of this grace, by believing with certainty that God will give it us, by surrendering ourselves up to it for the sake of the perishing world, desire may be strengthened. The first step will have been taken toward the possession of the coveted blessing. Let us seek the grace of prayer, as we seek "with our whole desire" the God with whom it will link us. We may depend upon the promise, "He fulfills the desire of all who fear him." Let us not fear to say to Him, "I desire it with my whole heart."

2. "What things soever ye desire, when *ye pray*." The desire of the heart must become the expression of the lips. Our Lord Jesus more than once asked those who cried to Him for mercy, "What wilt thou?" He wanted them to say what they desired. To declare it roused their whole being into action, brought them into contact with Him, and wakened their expectation. To pray is to enter into God's presence, to claim and secure His attention, to have distinct dealing with Him in regard to some request, to commit our need to His faithfulness and to leave it there. It is in so doing that we become fully conscious of what we are seeking.

There are some who often carry strong desires in their heart without bringing them to God in a clear expression of definite and repeated prayer. There are others who go to the Word and its promises to strengthen their faith but who do not give sufficient place to that pointed asking of God which helps the soul gain the assurance that the matter has been put into God's hands. Still others come in prayer with so many requests and desires that it is difficult for they themselves to say what they really expect God to do.

If you want God to give you this great gift of faithfulness in prayer and power to pray aright, begin to pray about it. Declare to yourself and to God, "Here is something I have asked, and am continuing to ask till I receive. As plain and pointed as words can make it, I am saying, 'My Father! I do desire, I do ask of you, and expect of you, the grace of prayer and intercession.' "

3. "What things soever ye desire, when ye pray, *believe*." It is only by faith that we can know God or receive Jesus Christ or live the Christian life. So also faith is the life and power of prayer. If we are to begin a life of intercession in which there is to be joy and power and blessing, if we are to have our prayer for the grace of prayer answered, we must learn anew what faith is, and begin to live and pray in faith as never before.

Faith is the opposite of sight, and the two are contrary to each other. "We walk by faith, and not by sight." If the unseen is to get full possession of us; and heart and life and prayer are to be full of faith, there must be a withdrawal from, a denial of, the visible. The spirit that seeks to enjoy as much as possible of what is innocent or legitimate, that gives the first place to the calls and duties of daily life, is inconsistent with a strong faith and close relationship with the spiritual world. "We *look not* at the things which are seen"—the negative action needs to be emphasized if the positive, "but at the things which are not seen," is to become natural to us. In praying, faith depends upon our living in the invisible world.

This faith refers especially to faith in God. The great reason for our lack of faith is our lack of knowledge of God and communion with Him. "Have faith in God," Jesus said when He spoke of removing mountains. When a soul knows God, is occupied with His power, love, and faithfulness, comes away out of self and the world, and allows the light of God to illuminate, unbelief will become impossible. All the mysteries and difficulties connected with answers to prayer will—however little we may be able to solve them intellectually—be swallowed up in the adoring assurance: "This God is our God. He will bless us. He does indeed answer prayer. And the grace to pray, that I am asking for, He will delight to give" (Appendix 3).

4. "What things soever ye desire, when ye pray, believe that *ye receive them. Faith has to accept the answer, as given by God in heaven, before it is found or felt upon earth.* This point causes difficulty, but it is the essence of believing prayer, its real secret. Try to understand. Spiritual things can only be spiritually grasped or appropriated. The spiritual heavenly blessing of God's answer to your prayer must be recognized and accepted in your spirit before you feel anything of it. It is faith which does this.

A person who not only seeks an answer, but seeks first the God who gives the answer, receives the power to know that he has obtained what he has asked of God. If he knows that he has asked according to God's will and promises, and that he has come to and found God to give it, he does believe that he has received. "We know that he heareth us."

There is nothing so heart searching as this faith, *"Believe that ye have received.*" As we strive to believe, and find we cannot, it leads us to discover what there is that hinders. Blessed is the man who holds nothing back and lets nothing hold him back. Instead with his eye and heart on God alone, he refuses to rest till he has believed what our Lord bids him, "that he has received." Here is the place where Jacob becomes Israel, and the power of prevailing prayer is born out of human weakness and despair. Here enters the real need for persevering and ever-importunate prayer that will not rest or go away or give up till it knows it is heard, and believes that it has received.

Are you praying for "the Spirit of grace and supplication"? As you ask for it in strong desire and believe in God who hears prayer, do not be afraid to persevere and believe that your life can indeed be changed. Believe that all the pressures of daily life which hinder prayer can be overcome. Believe that God will give you your heart's desire—grace to pray much and in His spirit, just as the Father would have His child do. "Believe that ye receive them."

5. "What things soever ye desire, when ye pray, believe that ye receive them, and *ye shall have them.*" The receiving from God in faith, the believing acceptance of the answer with the perfect and praising assurance that it has been given, is not necessarily the experience itself or subjective possession of the gift we have asked for. At times there may be a considerable or even a long interval. In other cases the believing supplicant may at once enjoy what he has received. Especially in the former case we have need of faith and patience. We need faith to rejoice in the assurance of the answer bestowed and received, and to begin to act upon that answer though nothing be felt. We need patience to wait even though for the present there is no visible proof of its presence. We can count upon the actual future enjoyment: "*Ye shall have.*"

We can apply this principle to our prayer for power to be faithful intercessors, for grace to pray earnestly and perseveringly for souls around us. Learn to hold fast the divine assurance that as surely as we believe, we receive. Believe that faith, therefore, apart from all failing, may rejoice in the certainty of an answered prayer. The more we praise God for it, the sooner will the experience come. We may begin at once to pray for others, in the confidence that grace will be given us to pray with more perseverance and more faith than we have done before.

If we do not find any immediate increase in our desire to pray or our power in prayer, this must not hinder or discourage us. Without feeling, we have accepted a divine spiritual gift by faith; in that faith we are to pray, doubting nothing. The Holy Spirit for a little while may hide himself within us. But we may count upon Him to pray in us, even though it be with groanings which cannot find expression. In due time we shall become conscious of His presence and power. As sure as there is desire and prayer and faith, and faith's acceptance of the gift, there will also be the manifestation and experience of the blessing we asked for.

Do you really want God to enable you to pray so that your life may be free from constant self-condemnation, and so that the power of His Spirit may come down in answer to your petition? Come and *ask it of God*. Kneel down and pray for it in a single definite sentence. When you have done so, kneel still in faith, believing in God who answers. Now believe that you are receiving what you have prayed; believe that you have received. If you find it difficult to do this, continue kneeling, and say that you believe it on the strength of His own word. If it cost time, and struggle, and doubt, fear not. At His feet as you look up into His face, faith will come.

"Believe that ye receive." At His bidding you dare claim the answer. Begin in that faith, even though it be feeble, a new prayer life, with this one thought as its strength: You have asked and received grace from Christ to prepare you, step by step, to be faithful in prayer and intercession. The more simply you hold to this and expect the Holy Spirit to work it in you, the more surely and fully will the word be made true to you. "Ye shall have them." God himself who gave the answer will work it in you.

CHAPTER TEN

The Spirit of Supplication

"I will pour upon the house of David . . . the spirit of grace and of supplication" (Zech. 12:10).

"The Spirit also helpeth our infirmities; for we know not what we should pray for as we ought: but the Spirit himself maketh intercession for us with groanings which cannot be uttered. And he that searcheth the hearts knoweth what is the mind of the Spirit, because he maketh intercession for the saints according to the will of God" (Rom. 8:26, 27).

"Praying always with all prayer and supplication in the Spirit, and watching thereunto with all perseverance and supplication for all saints" (Eph. 6:18).

"Praying in the Holy Spirit" (Jude 20).

The Holy Spirit has been given to every child of God to be his life. He dwells in him, not as a separate being in one part of his nature, but as his very life. He is the divine power or energy by which his life is maintained and strengthened. All that a believer is called to be or to do, the Holy Spirit can and will work in him. If a person does not know or yield to the Holy Guest, the Blessed Spirit cannot work, and his life is a sickly one, full of failure and of sin. As he yields, waits, and then obeys the leading of the Spirit, God works in him all that is pleasing in His sight.

This Holy Spirit is, in the first place, a Spirit of prayer. He was promised as a "Spirit of grace and supplication" the grace for supplication. He was sent forth into our hearts as the "Spirit of adoption, whereby we cry, Abba, Father." He enables us to say, in true faith and growing understanding of its meaning, "Our Father which art in heaven."

"He maketh intercession for the saints according to the will of God." As we pray in the Spirit, our worship is as God seeks it to be, "in spirit and in truth." Prayer is simply the breathing of the Spirit in us; power in prayer comes from the power of the Spirit in us as we wait on and trust Him. Failure in prayer comes from feebleness of the Spirit's work in us. Our prayer is a gauge that measures the Spirit's work within us. To pray in the right way, the life of the Spirit must be right in us. For praying the effective, much-availing prayer of the righteous man everything depends on being full of the Spirit.

The believer who would enjoy the blessing of being taught to pray by the Spirit of prayer must know four very simple lessons. The first is: *Believe that the Spirit dwells in you* (Eph. 1:13). Deep in the inmost recesses of his being, hidden and unfelt, every child of God has the holy, mighty Spirit of God dwelling in him. He knows it by faith, the faith that, by accepting God's word, lays hold on that of which he sees as yet no sign.

"We . . . receive the promise of the Spirit through faith." As long as we measure our power, to pray persistently and in the right way, by what we feel or think we can accomplish, we shall be discouraged when we hear of how much we ought to pray. But when we quietly believe that the Holy Spirit as a spirit of supplication is dwelling within us in the middle of all our conscious weakness, *for the very purpose of enabling us to pray in such manner and measure as God would have us,* our hearts will be filled with hope. We shall be strengthened in the assurance which lies at the very root of a happy and fruitful Christian life that *God has made abundant provision for our being what He wants us to be.* We shall begin to lose our sense of burden and fear and discouragement about our ever praying sufficiently, because we see that the Holy Spirit himself will pray and is praying in us.

The second lesson is: *Beware above everything of grieving the Holy Spirit* (Eph. 4:30). If you do, how can He work in you the quiet, trustful, and blessed sense of that union with Christ which makes your prayers well pleasing to the Father? Beware of grieving Him by sin, by unbelief, by selfishness, by unfaithfulness to His voice in your conscience.

Do not think that grieving Him is a necessity. That idea cuts away the very sinews of your strength to obey the command. Do not consider it impossible to obey the words, "grieve not the Holy Spirit." He himself is the very power of God to make you obedient. Sins that rise up in you against your will, a tendency to sloth, pride, self-will, or passion that rises in the flesh, your will can at once reject in the power of the Spirit and cast them upon Christ and His blood. Then your communion with God is immediately restored.

Accept each day the Holy Spirit as your leader and life and strength; you can count upon Him to do in your heart all that ought to be done there. He, the unseen and unfelt one but known by faith, gives there, unseen and unfelt, the love and the faith and the power of obedience you need. He reveals Christ unseen within you, as your life and strength. Do not grieve the Holy Spirit by distrusting Him, simply because you do not feel His presence in you.

Especially in the matter of prayer do not grieve the Spirit. When you trust Christ to bring you into a new, healthy prayer life, do not expect that you will be able all at once to pray as easily and powerfully and joyfully as you want to do. These things may not come immediately. Just bow quietly before God in your ignorance and weakness. The best and truest prayer is to put yourself before God just as you are and to count on the hidden Spirit praying in you.

"We know not what we should pray for as we ought"; ignorance, difficulty, struggle mark our prayer all along. But, "the Spirit also helpeth our infirmities." How? "The Spirit itself," deeper down than our thoughts or feelings, "maketh intercession for us with groanings which cannot be uttered." When you cannot find words, when your words appear cold and feeble, just believe, *the Holy Spirit is praying in me.*

Be quiet before God, and give Him time and opportunity. In due season you will learn to pray. Beware of grieving the Spirit of prayer by not honoring Him in patient, trustful surrender to His intercession in you.

The third lesson: *"Be filled with the Spirit"* (Eph. 5:18). I think that we have seen the meaning of the great truth: It is only the healthy spiritual life that can pray as it should. The command comes to each of us: "Be filled with the Spirit." That implies that even though some may rest content with only the beginning and with a small measure of the Spirit's working, it is God's will that we should be filled with the Spirit. From our side that means that our whole being ought to be entirely yielded up to the Holy Spirit, to be possessed and controlled by Him alone.

From God's side, we may count upon and expect the Holy Spirit to take possession and fill us.

Our failure in prayer evidently has been due to our not having accepted the Spirit of prayer to be our life; to our having failed to yield wholly to Him whom the Father gave as the Spirit of His Son, so that He might work the life of the Son in us. Let us be willing to receive Him, to yield ourselves to God and trust Him to fill us. Let us not again willfully grieve the Holy Spirit by declining, neglecting, or hesitating to seek to have Him as fully as He is willing to give himself to us. If we have seen that prayer is the great need of our work and of the Church, if we have desired or resolved to pray more, let us turn to the very source of all power and blessing. Let us believe that the Spirit of prayer in His fullness is for us.

We all agree as to the place the Father and the Son have in our prayer. It is to the Father we pray, and from whom we expect the answer. It is in the merit, the name, and life of the Son, by our abiding in Him and He in us, that we trust to be heard. But have we understood that in the Holy Trinity all the three persons have an equal place in prayer? Faith in the Holy Spirit of intercession as He prays in us is as indispensable as the faith in the Father and the Son. How clearly we have this in the words, "Through [Christ] we both have access by one Spirit unto the Father." As much as prayer must be *to* the Father, and *through* the Son, it must be *by* the Spirit. And the Spirit can pray in no other way in us than as He lives in us. It is only as we yield ourselves to the Spirit living and praying in us that the glory of the prayer-hearing God and the ever-blessed and most effective mediation of the Son can be known by us in their power (Appendix 4).

Our final lesson: *Pray in the Spirit for all saints* (Eph. 6:18). The Spirit, who is called the Spirit of supplication, is also and very specially the Spirit of intercession. It is said of Him, "The Spirit itself maketh intercession for us with groanings which cannot be uttered." "He maketh intercession for the saints." It is the same word as is used of Christ, "who also maketh intercession for us."

The thought in the above verses is essentially that of mediation—one person pleading for another. When the Spirit of intercession takes full possession of us, all selfishness—of wanting Him separate from His intercession for others and just for ourselves alone—is banished, and we begin to avail ourselves of our wonderful privilege to plead for men. We long to live the Christ-life of self-consuming sacrifice for others. Our heart unceasingly yields itself to God to obtain His blessing for those around us. Intercession then becomes, not an incident or an occasional part of our prayers, but their one great object. Prayer for ourselves then takes its true place as a mere means of preparing us better so we can be more effective in the exercise of our ministry of intercession.

I have humbly asked God to give me that I may give you divine light and help to forsake the life of failure in prayer, and to enter at once upon the life of intercession which the Holy Spirit can enable you to lead. By a simple act of faith claim the fullness of the Spirit in the full measure you are capable in God's sight of receiving and which He is therefore willing to bestow. Will you not, even now, receive this by faith?

What takes place at conversion? Most of you for a time sought peace by struggling to give up sin and please God. But you did not find it that way. The peace of God's pardon came by faith, by trusting God's Word concerning Christ and His salvation. You had heard of Christ as the gift of God's love, you knew that He was for you too and you had felt the movings and drawings of His grace. But never until by faith in God's Word you accepted Christ as God's gift to you did you know the peace and joy that He can give. Believing in Him and His saving love made all the difference and changed your relation from one who had always grieved Him to one who now loved and served Him. Yet you have a thousand times wondered that you love and serve Him far less than He deserves.

At the time of your conversion you knew little about the Holy Spirit. Later on you heard of His dwelling in you and His being the power of God in you for all the Father intends you to be. In spite of that, His indwelling and inworking have been something vague and indefinite, hardly a source of joy or strength. At conversion you did not yet know your need of Him and still less what you might expect of Him. But your failures have taught it to you. Now you begin to see how you have been grieving Him by not trusting and not following Him, by not allowing Him to work in you all God's pleasure.

All this can be changed. After seeking Christ, and praying to Him, and trying without success to serve Him, you found rest in accepting Him by faith. Even so you may now yield yourself to the full guidance of the Holy Spirit, and claim and accept Him to work in you what God would have. Will you do it? Accept Him in faith as Christ's gift to be the Spirit of your whole life, including your prayer life. You can count upon Him to take charge. No matter how feeble or unable to pray aright you feel, you can bow before God in silence, with the assurance that He will teach you to pray.

Just as you by conscious faith accepted Christ's pardon, you can now consciously receive in faith the Holy Spirit whom Christ gives to do His work in you. "Christ hath redeemed us . . . that we might receive the promise of the Spirit by faith." Kneel down, and simply believe that the Lord Christ, who baptizes with the Holy Spirit, now, in response to your faith, will begin in you the blessed life of a full experience of the power of the indwelling Spirit. Depend most confidently upon Him, apart from all feeling or experience, as the spirit of supplication and intercession to do His work. Renew that act of faith each morning, each time you pray. Trust Him, against all appearances, to work in you— be assured He is working—and He will reveal to you the joy of the Holy Spirit as the power of your life.

"I will pour . . . the spirit of grace and of supplication." The mystery of prayer is the mystery of the divine indwelling. God in heaven gives His Spirit in our hearts to be there the divine power praying in us and drawing us upward to our God. God is a Spirit, and nothing but a like life and Spirit within us can have communion with Him.

It was for communion man was created that God might dwell and work in man and be the life of his life. It was this divine indwelling that sin lost. It was this that Christ came to exhibit in His life, to win back for us in His death, and then to impart to us by coming again from heaven in the Spirit to live in His disciples. It is this indwelling of God through the Spirit that alone can explain and enable us to appropriate the wonderful promises given to prayer. God gives the Spirit as a spirit of supplication, also, to maintain His divine life within us as a life out of which prayer continually rises upward.

Without the Holy Spirit no man can call Jesus Lord, or cry, "Abba, Father"; no man can worship in spirit and truth, or pray without ceasing. The Holy Spirit is given to the believer to be and do in him all that God wants him to be or do. He is given Him especially as the Spirit of prayer and supplication. It is clear that everything in prayer depends upon our trusting the Holy Spirit to do His work in us, yielding ourselves to His leading, depending only and wholly on Him.

We read that Stephen was "a man full of faith and the Holy Spirit." The two always go together, in exact proportion to each other. As our faith sees and trusts the Spirit in us to pray, and waits on Him, He will do His work. It is the longing desire, the earnest supplication, and the definite faith the Father seeks. Let us know Him, and in the faith of Christ who unceasingly gives Him, cultivate the assured confidence that we *can* learn to pray as the Father would have us.

CHAPTER ELEVEN

In the Name of Christ

"Whatsoever ye shall ask *in my name*, that will I do. . . . If ye shall ask any thing *in my name*, I will do it. . . . I have chosen you, and ordained you, that whatsoever ye shall ask of the Father *in my name*, he may give it you. . . . Verily, verily I say unto you, Whatsoever ye shall ask the Father *in my name*, he will give it you. Hitherto have ye asked nothing *in my name*: ask, and ye shall receive, that your joy may be full. . . . At that day ye shall ask *in my name*" (John 14:13; 15:16; 16:23, 24, 26).

"In my name" is repeated six times in our text. Our Lord knew how slow our hearts would be to take it in, but He so longed that we should really believe that His name is the power in which every knee should bow, and in which every prayer could be heard. He did not weary of saying over and over, "In my name"! Between the wonderful "whatsoever ye shall ask" and the divine "I will do it, the Father will give it" is the simple link, "In my name." Our asking and the Father's giving are to be equally in the name of Christ. Everything in prayer depends upon our grasping this—"In my name."

A name is a word by which we call up to our mind the whole being and nature of an object. When I speak of a lamb or a lion, the name at once suggests the nature peculiar to each. The name of God is meant to express His whole divine nature and glory. So also the name of Christ means His whole nature, His person and work, His disposition and Spirit. To ask in the name of Christ is to pray in union with Him.

When a sinner first believes in Christ, he knows and thinks only of His merit and intercession—and to the very end that is the one foundation of our confidence. But as the believer grows in grace and enters more deeply and truly into union with Christ—

as he abides in Him—he learns that to pray in the name of Christ also means in His Spirit and in the possession of His nature, as the Holy Spirit imparts it to us.

As we grasp the meaning of the words, "At that day ye shall ask in my name"—the day when in the Holy Spirit Christ came to live in His disciples—we shall no longer be staggered at the greatness of the promise: *"Whatsoever* ye shall ask in my name, that will I do." We shall get some insight into the unchangeable necessity and certainty of the law: *What is asked in the name of Christ, in union with Him, out of His nature and Spirit, must be given.*

As Christ's prayer-nature lives in us, His prayer-power becomes ours too. The measure of our attainment or experience will not be the ground of our confidence. Rather, the honesty and wholeheartedness of our surrender to all that we see that Christ seeks to be in us will be the measure of our spiritual fitness and power to pray in His name. "If ye abide in me," He says, "ye shall ask what ye will."

As we live in Him, we receive the spiritual power to avail ourselves of His name. As the branch wholly given up to the life and service of the Vine can count upon all its sap and strength for its fruit, so the believer, who in faith has accepted the fullness of the Spirit to possess his whole life, can indeed avail himself of all the power of Christ's name.

Here on earth Christ as man came to reveal what prayer is. To pray in the name of Christ we must pray as He prayed on earth. He taught us to pray in union with Him, as He now prays in heaven. We must in love study, and in faith accept Him as our example, our teacher, our intercessor.

Christ Our Example

Prayer in Christ on earth and in us cannot be two different things. Just as there is but one God, who is a Spirit, who hears prayer, there is but one spirit of acceptable prayer. We must realize how much time Christ spent in prayer, and how the great events of His life were all connected with special prayer. Then we learn the necessity of absolute dependence on and unceasing direct communication with the heavenly world if we are to live a heavenly life, or to exercise heavenly power around us.

We see how foolish and fruitless the attempt must be to do work for God and heaven without in the first place in prayer getting the life and the power of heaven to possess us. Unless this truth lives in us, we cannot avail ourselves aright of the mighty power of the name of Christ. His example must teach us the meaning of His name.

Of His baptism we read, "Jesus also being baptized, *and praying*, the heaven was opened." It was in prayer heaven was opened to Him, and that heaven came down to Him with the Spirit and the voice of the Father. In the power of these He was led into the wilderness, in fasting and prayer, to have them tested, and fully appropriated.

Early in Jesus' ministry Mark records (1:35), "And in the morning rising up a great while before day, he went out, and departed into a solitary place, *and there prayed*." Somewhat later Luke tells us (5:16), "Multitudes came together to hear and to be healed. . . . *And he withdrew himself into the wilderness, and prayed*."

Jesus knew how even the holiest service of preaching and healing can exhaust the spirit, how too much contact with men can cloud the fellowship with God. He knew that much time is needed if the spirit is to rest and take root in Him. He recognized that no pressure of duty among men can free from the absolute need of much prayer.

If anyone could have been satisfied with always living and working in the Spirit of prayer, it would have been our Master. But He could not; He needed to have His supplies replenished by continual and lengthy seasons of prayer. To use Christ's name in prayer surely includes following His example and to pray as He did.

About the night before choosing His apostles we read (Luke 6:12), "He went into a mountain *to pray, and continued all night in prayer to God*." The first step toward the establishment of the Church, and the separation of men to be His witnesses and successors, required special long-continued prayer. All had to be done according to the pattern Jesus revealed: "The Son can do nothing of himself . . . but what he seeth the Father do." It was in the night of prayer it was shown Him.

84

In the night between the feeding of the five thousand, when Jesus knew that the people wanted to take Him by force and make Him king, and the walking on the sea, "He went up into a mountain apart *to pray*" (Matt. 14:23; Mark 6:46; John 6:15). He had come to do God's will and to show forth God's power. He did not have it as a possession of His own; it had to be prayed for and received from above.

The first announcement of Christ's approaching death, after He had drawn from Peter the confession that He was the Christ, is introduced by the words (Luke 9:18), "And it came to pass, as *he was alone praying*." The introduction to the story of the Transfiguration says (Luke 9:28), "He went up into a mountain *to pray*." The request of the disciples, "Lord, teach us to pray" (Luke 11:1), follows the statement, "It came to pass, that *as he was praying* in a certain place." In His own personal life, in His relationship with the Father, in all He is and does for men, the Christ whose name we are to use is a man of prayer.

It is prayer that gives Christ His power of blessing and transfigures His very body with the glory of heaven. It is His prayer life that qualifies Him to teach others how to pray. How much more must it be prayer, prayer alone, much prayer, that can fit us to share His glory of a transfigured life, or make us the channel of heavenly blessing and teaching to others. To pray in the name of Christ is to pray as He prays.

As Christ's death approached, He still prayed. When the Greeks asked to see Him, and He spoke of His approaching death, He prayed. At Lazarus' grave He prayed. In the last night He prayed His prayer as our High Priest that we might know what His sacrifice would win, and what His everlasting intercession on the throne would be. In Gethsemane He prayed His prayer as victim—the Lamb giving itself to the slaughter. On the Cross it is still all prayer—the prayer of compassion for His murderers, the prayer of atoning suffering in the thick darkness, the prayer in death of confident resignation of His spirit to the Father (Appendix 5).

Christ's life and work, His suffering and death, were founded on prayer, total dependence on God, trust in God, receiving from God, surrender to God. Your redemption is a redemption brought into being by prayer and intercession. Your Christ is a praying

Christ. The life He lived *for* you, the life He lives *in* you, is a praying life that delights to wait on God and receive all from Him. To pray in His name is to pray as He prayed. Christ is only our example because He is our Head, our Savior, and our Life. In virtue of His deity and of His Spirit, He can live in us. We can pray in His name because we abide in Him and He abides in us.

Christ Our Teacher

Christ was what He taught. All His teaching was simply the revelation of how He lived, and—praise God—of the life He was to live in us. His teaching of the disciples was first to awaken desire, and so prepare them for what He would by the Holy Spirit be and work in them. Let us believe very confidently that all He was in prayer, and all that He taught, He himself will give. He came to fulfill the law; much more will He fulfill the gospel in all that He taught us, as to what to pray, and how.

1. *What to pray.* It has sometimes been said that direct petitions, as compared with the exercise of fellowship with God, are but a subordinate part of prayer, and that "in the prayer of those who pray best and most, they occupy but an inconsiderable place." If we carefully study all that our Lord spoke of prayer, we shall see that this is not His teaching. In the Lord's Prayer; in the parables on prayer; in the illustration of a child asking bread, of our seeking and knocking, in the central thought of the prayer of faith, "Whatsoever ye shall ask in prayer, believing ye shall receive"; in the oft-repeated *"whatsoever"* of the last evening—everywhere—our Lord urges and encourages us to offer definite petitions, and to expect definite answers.

Only because we have too much confined prayer to our own needs has it been thought necessary to free it from the appearance of selfishness by giving the petitions a subordinate place. Believers need to wake up to the glory of the work of intercession. They need to see that in it and in the definite pleading for definite gifts on definite spheres and persons lie our highest fellowship with our glorified Lord, and our only real power to bless men. Then it would be clear that there can be no truer fellowship with God than these definite petitions and their answers, by which we become the channel of His grace and life to men. Then our fellowship with the Father can be such as the Son has in His intercession.

2. *How to pray.* Our Lord taught us to pray in secret, in simplicity, with the eye on God alone, in humility, in the spirit of forgiving love. But the chief truth He reiterated was always this: *pray in faith.* He defined faith not only as a trust in God's goodness or power but as the definite assurance that we have received the very thing we ask. Then, in view of the delay in the answer, he insisted on perseverance and urgency.

We must be followers of those "who through faith and patience inherit the promises." We musn't exercise the faith that accepts the promise and knows it has what it has asked, and practice the patience that obtains the promise and inherits the blessing. We shall then learn to understand why God, who promises to avenge His elect speedily, bears with them in seeming delay. It is that their faith may be purified from all that is of the flesh, and tested and strengthened to become that spiritual power that can do all things—that can even cast mountains into the heart of the sea.

Christ as Our Intercessor

We have observed Christ in His prayers and we have listened to His teaching as to how we must pray. But to know fully what it is to pray in His name, we must know Him too in His heavenly intercession.

Consider that all Christ's saving work accomplished from heaven is still carried on, just as it was on earth, in unceasing communication with, and direct intercession to, the Father, who works all in all, who is All in All. Every act of grace in Christ has been preceded by, and owes its power to, intercession. God has been honored and acknowledged as its Author.

On the throne of God, Christ's highest fellowship with the Father and His partnership in His rule of the world is in intercession. Every blessing that comes down to us from above bears upon it the stamp from God, through Christ's intercession. His intercession is the fruit and the glory of His atonement. When He gave himself a sacrifice to God for men, He proved that His whole heart had one object—the glory of God in the salvation of men. In His intercession this great purpose is realized: He glorifies the Father by asking and receiving all from Him, and He saves men by bestowing what He has obtained from the Father. Christ's intercession is the Father's glory, His own glory, our glory.

This Christ, the Intercessor, is our life, He is our Head and we are His body. His Spirit and life breathe in us. As in heaven so on earth, intercession is God's chosen, God's only channel of blessing. Let us learn from Christ what glory there is in this. What is the way to exercise this wondrous power? What is the part it is to take in work for God?

1. *The glory of intercession.* By it, beyond anything, we glorify God. By it we glorify Christ. By it we bring blessing to the Church and the world. By it we obtain our highest nobility—the godlike power of saving men.

2. *The way to intercession.* Paul writes, "Walk in love, as Christ also hath loved us, and hath given himself for us an offering and a sacrifice to God." If we live as Christ lived, we will, as He did, give ourselves for our whole life to God to be used by Him for men. When once we have done this and given ourselves to God, no more to seek anything for ourselves but for men, for God to use us, and to give us what we can bestow on others, then intercession will become to us—as it is in Christ in heaven—the great work of our life.

If ever the thought comes that the call is too high or the work too great, the faith in Christ, the interceding Christ who lives in us, will give us the victory. We will listen to Him who said, "The works that I do, shall he do also; and greater works than these shall he do." We shall remember that we are not under the law with its impotence, but under grace with its omnipotence, working all in us. We shall believe again in Him who said to us, "Rise and walk," and gave us—and we received it—His life as our strength. We shall claim afresh the fullness of God's Spirit as His sufficient provision for our need. We shall count Him to be in us the Spirit of intercession who makes us one with Christ in His fullness. Let us only stand firm, giving up ourselves, like Him, in Him, to God for men.

Then we shall understand the part intercession is to take in God's work through us. We shall no longer try to work for God and ask Him to follow it with His blessing. We shall do what the friend at midnight did, what Christ did on earth, and ever does in heaven—we shall first get from God and then turn to men to give what He gave us.

As with Christ, we shall make it our chief work to receive from the Father. We shall count no time or trouble too great. Our giving to men will then be in power.

Be of good courage as servants of Christ and children of God. Let no fear of feebleness or poverty make you afraid—ask in the name of Christ. His name is himself, in all His perfection and power. He is the living Christ, and will himself make His name a power in you. Do not fear to plead in His name. His promise is a threefold cord that cannot be broken: *"Whatsoever ye ask—in my name—it shall be done unto you."*

CHAPTER TWELVE

My God Will Hear Me

"Therefore will the Lord wait, that he may be gracious unto you. . . . Blessed are all they that wait for him. He will be very gracious unto thee at the voice of thy cry; when he shall hear it, he will answer thee" (Isa. 30:18, 19).

"The Lord will hear when *I call* unto him" (Ps. 4:3).

"I have called upon thee, for thou *wilt hear me*, O God" (Ps. 17:6).

"I will look unto the Lord; I will wait for the God of my salvation: my God *will hear me*" (Mic. 7:7).

The power of prayer rests in the faith that God hears prayer. In more than one sense this is true. It is this faith that gives a man courage to pray. It is this faith that gives him power to prevail with God. The moment I am assured that God hears *me* too, I feel drawn to pray and to persevere in prayer. I feel strong to claim and to take in faith the answer God gives. One great reason for lack of prayer is the want of the living, joyous assurance, "My God will hear me." If only God's servants would get a vision of the living God waiting to grant their request and to bestow all the heavenly gifts of the Spirit they are in need of either for themselves or those they are serving. Then they would set aside everything to make time and room for this one and only power that can insure heavenly blessing—the prayer of faith!

When a man can and does say in living faith, "My God will hear me!" surely nothing can keep him from prayer. He knows that what he cannot do on earth can and will be done for him from heaven. Let each one of us bow in stillness before God, and wait on Him to reveal himself as the prayer-hearing God. In His presence the wondrous thoughts gathering round the central truth will unfold themselves to us.

1. *"My God will hear me." What a blessed certainty!* We

have God's Word for it in many promises. We have thousands of witnesses to the fact that they have found it true. We have had experience of it in our lives. We have had the Son of God come from heaven with the message that if we ask, the Father will give. We have had Christ praying on earth and being heard. Now we have Him in heaven sitting at the right hand of God and making intercession for us. God hears prayer—God *delights* to hear prayer. He has allowed His people a thousand times over to be tried that they might be compelled to cry to Him, and learn to know Him as the Hearer of Prayer.

Let us confess with shame how little we have believed this wondrous truth, in actually receiving it into our heart and allowing it to possess and control our whole being. Accepting a truth is not enough; the living God, of whom the truth speaks, must in its light so be revealed that our whole life is spent in His presence. We must live with an awareness as clear as in a little child toward its earthly parent—I know for certain my father hears me.

By experience you know how little an intellectual understanding of truth has profited you. Ask God to reveal himself to you. If you want to live a different prayer life, bow each time before you pray in silence to worship this God. Wait there until there rests on you a deep consciouness of His nearness and His readiness to answer. After that you can begin to pray with the words, "My God will hear me!"

2. *"My God will hear me." What a wondrous grace!* Think of God in His infinite majesty, His altogether incomprehensible glory, His unapproachable holiness, sitting on a throne of grace, waiting to be gracious, inviting and encouraging you to pray with His promise: "Call unto me, and I will answer thee."

Think of yourself, in your nothingness and helplessness as a creature; in your wretchedness and transgressions as a sinner; in your feebleness and unworthiness as a saint; and praise the glory of that grace which allows you to say boldly of your prayer for yourself and others, "My God will hear me."

Think of what you can accomplish, in this wonderful intimacy with God. God has united you with Christ. In Him and His name you have your confidence. On the throne He prays with you and for you. On the footstool of the throne you pray with Him and in Him. His worth and the Father's delight in hearing Him are the measure of your confidence, your assurance of being heard.

There is more. When you know not what to pray as you ought, think of the Holy Spirit, the Spirit of God's own Son, sent into your heart to cry, "Abba, Father," and to be *in you* a Spirit of supplication. Think, in all your insignificance and unworthiness, of your being as acceptable as Christ himself. Think, in all your ignorance and weakness, of the Spirit making intercession according to God within you, and cry out, "What wondrous grace! Through Christ I have access to the Father, by the Spirit. I can, I do believe it: 'My God will hear me.' "

3. *"My God will hear me." What a deep mystery!* There are difficulties that at times arise and perplex even the honest heart. There is the question as to God's sovereign will. How can our wishes, often so foolish, and our will, often so selfish, overrule or change that perfect will? Would it not be better to leave all to His disposal, who knows what is best, and loves to give us the very best? Or how can our prayer change what He has ordained before?

The question arises, too, as to the need of persevering prayer, and long waiting for the answer. If God be infinite love, and delighting more to give than we to receive, why is there need for pleading and wrestling, or the urgency, and long delay of which Scripture and experience speak?

Arising out of this there is still another question—that of the multitude of apparently vain and unanswered prayers. How many have pleaded for loved ones and they die unsaved. How many cry for years for spiritual blessing and no answer comes. To think of all this tries our faith, and makes us hesitate as we say, "My God will hear me."

Prayer, in its power with God, and His faithfulness to His promise to hear it, is a deep spiritual mystery. Answers can be given that remove some of the difficulty from the questions asked above. But, after all, the first and the last that must be said is this: As little as we can comprehend God can we comprehend one of the most blessed of His attributes—that He hears prayer. It is a spiritual mystery—nothing less than the mystery of the Holy Trinity.

God hears because we pray in His Son, because the Holy Spirit prays in us. If we have believed and claimed the life of Christ as our health, and the fullness of the Spirit as our strength, let us not hesitate to believe in the power of our prayer too. The Holy Spirit can enable us to believe and rejoice in it, even where every question is not yet answered. He will do this, as we surrender our questions to God's love, trust His faithfulness, and give ourselves humbly to obey His command to pray without ceasing.

Every art unfolds its secrets and its beauty only to the man who practices it. To the humble soul who prays in the obedience of faith, who practices prayer and intercession diligently because God asks it, the secret of the Lord will be revealed. Then the thought of the deep mystery of prayer, instead of being a weary problem, will be a source of rejoicing, adoration and faith, in which the unceasing refrain is ever heard, *"My God will hear me."*

4. *"My God will hear me." What a solemn responsibility!* Often we complain of darkness, of feebleness, of failure, as if there was no help for it. Yet God has promised in answer to our prayer to supply our every need and give us His light and strength and peace. If only we could realize the responsibility of having such a God and such promises and see the sin and shame of not availing ourselves of them to the utmost. How confident we should feel that the grace, which we have accepted and trusted to enable us to pray as we should, will be given.

This access to a prayer-hearing God is especially meant to make us intercessors for our fellowmen. Christ obtained His right of prevailing intercession by His giving himself as a sacrifice to God for men, and through it receives the blessings He dispenses. Even so, if we have truly with Christ given ourselves to God for men, we share Christ's right of intercession, and are able to obtain the powers of the heavenly world for men also.

The power of life and death is in our hands (1 John 5:16). In answer to prayer, the Spirit can be poured out, souls can be converted, believers can be established. In prayer, the kingdom of darkness can be conquered, souls brought out of prison into the liberty of Christ, and the glory of God be revealed. Through prayer, the sword of the Spirit, which is the Word of God, can be wielded in power; in public preaching as well as in private speaking, the most rebellious can be made to bow at Jesus' feet.

What a responsibility on the Church to give herself to the

work of intercession! What a responsibility on every minister, missionary and worker, set apart for the saving of souls, to yield himself wholly to act out and prove his faith: "My God will hear me!" What a call on every believer—instead of burying and losing this talent—to seek to the very utmost to use it in prayer and supplication for all saints and for all men. "My God will hear me." The deeper our entrance into the truth of this wonderful power God has given to men, the more wholehearted will be our surrender to the work of intercession.

5. *"My God will hear me." What a blessed prospect!* I see now that all the failures of my past life have been due to lack of this faith. Especially in the work of intercession, my failure has had its deepest root in this—I did not live in the full faith of the blessed assurance, *"My God will hear me!"* Praise God! I begin to see it and I believe it. All can be different. Or, rather, I see *Him*, I believe *Him, "My God will hear me!"* Yes, even me.

Commonplace and insignificant though I be and filling but a very little place, so that I will scarcely be missed when I go—even I have access to this infinite God, with the confidence that He hears me. One with Christ and led by the Holy Spirit, I dare to say, "I will pray for others, for I am sure my God will listen to me; 'My God will hear me.' "

What a blessed prospect before me—every earthly and spiritual anxiety exchanged for the peace of God, who cares for all and hears prayer. What a blessed prospect in my work—to know that even when the answer is long delayed and there is a call for much patient, persevering prayer, the truth remains infallibly sure— "My God will hear me."

What a blessed prospect for Christ's Church if only we could all give prayer its place, give faith in God its place, or, rather, *give the prayer-hearing God His place*! Is not this the one great thing, that those who begin to awaken to the urgent need of prayer ought to pray for primarily?

When God at the first, time after time, poured forth the Spirit on His praying people, He laid down the law for all time: In the degree that you pray, so you receive of the Spirit. Let each one who can say, "My God will hear me," join in the fervent supplication that throughout the Church this truth may be restored to its true place and the blessed prospect will be realized: a praying

Church endued with the power of the Holy Spirit.

6. *"My God will hear me."* What a need of divine teaching! We need this both to enable us to hold this word in living faith and to make full use of it in intercession. It has been said—although it cannot be said too often or too earnestly—that the one thing needful for the Church of our day is the power of the Holy Spirit. Because this is so from the divine side, we may also say just as truthfully from the human side, the one thing needed is more prayer, more believing and more persevering prayer.

In speaking of lack of the Spirit's power, and the condition for receiving that power someone used the expression, "The block is not on the perpendicular, but on the horizontal line." It is to be feared that it is on both. There is much to be confessed and taken away in us if the Spirit is to work freely. But it is especially on the perpendicular line where the block is—the upward look, and the deep dependence, and the strong crying to God, and the effectual prayer of faith that avails—all these are sadly lacking. And these are just the things that are needed.

We must all strive to learn the lesson which will make prevailing prayer possible—the lesson of a faith that always sings, *"My God will hear me."* Simple and elementary as it is, it needs practice and patience, it needs time and heavenly teaching to learn this lesson well. Under the impression of a bright thought or a blessed experience, it may look as if we knew the lesson perfectly. But over and over the need will recur of making this our first prayer—that God who hears prayer would teach us to believe it, and so to pray as we should.

If we desire revelation we can count upon Him. He delights in hearing prayer and answering it. He gave His Son that He might ever pray for us and with us, and His Holy Spirit to pray in us. We can be sure there is not a prayer that He will hear more certainly than this: that He so reveal himself as the prayer-hearing God that our whole being may respond, *"My God will hear me."*

CHAPTER THIRTEEN

Paul, a Pattern of Prayer

"Go . . . and inquire . . . for one called Saul, of Tarsus: for, *behold, he prayeth*" (Acts 9:11).

"For this cause I obtained mercy, that in me first Jesus Christ might shew forth all longsuffering, for a pattern to them which should hereafter believe on him to life everlasting" (1 Tim. 1:16).

God took His own Son, and made Him our example and our pattern. Sometimes it seems as if the power of Christ's example is lost in the thought that He, in whom is no sin, is not man as we are.

Our Lord took Paul, a man of like passions with ourselves, and made him a pattern of what He could do for one who was the chief of sinners. And Paul, the man who, more than any other, has set his mark on the Church, has ever been appealed to as a pattern man.

In his mastery of divine truth and his teaching of it, in his devotion to his Lord and his self-consuming zeal in His service, in his deep experience of the power of the indwelling Christ and the fellowship of His cross, in the sincerity of his humility and the simplicity and boldness of his faith, in his missionary enthusiasm and endurance—in all this, and so much more, "the grace of our Lord was exceeding abundant" in him.

Christ gave Paul, and the Church has accepted him, as a pattern of what Christ would have, of what Christ would work. Seven times Paul speaks of believers following him: (1 Cor. 4:16), "Wherefore I beseech you, be ye followers of me"; (11:1), "Be ye followers of me, even as I also am of Christ"; Phil. 3:17, 4:9; 1 Thess. 1:6; 2 Thess. 3:7-9.

If Paul, as a pattern of prayer, is not as much studied or appealed to as he is in other respects, it is not because he is not a remarkable proof of what grace can do. Neither is it because we do not, in this respect, stand in need of the help of his example. A study of Paul as a pattern of prayer will bring a rich reward of instruction and encouragement.

The words our Lord used of him at his conversion, "Behold, he prayeth," may be taken as the keynote of Paul's life. The heavenly vision which brought him to his knees ever after ruled his life. Christ at the right hand of God, in whom we are blessed with all spiritual blessings, was everything to Paul. Prayer and expectation of heavenly power in his work and on his work, directly from heaven by prayer, was the simple outcome of Paul's faith in the Glorified One. In this, too, Christ meant him to be a pattern that we might learn that, exactly in the measure in which the heavenliness of Christ and His gifts and the unworldliness of the powers that work for salvation are known and believed will prayer become the spontaneous rising of the heart to the only source of its life. Let us see what we know of Paul.

Paul's Habits of Prayer

Paul reveals these almost unconsciously. He writes (Rom. 1:9, 11): "God is my witness . . . that without ceasing I make mention of you *always in my prayers.* For I long to see you, that I may impart unto you some spiritual gift, to the end ye may be established."

Rom. 10:1; 9:2, 3: "My *heart's desire and prayer to God* for Israel is, that they might be saved"; "I have great heaviness and *continual sorrow in my heart,* for I could wish that myself were accursed from Christ for my brethren."

1 Cor. 1:4: "I thank my God *always* on your behalf, for the grace of God which is given you by Jesus Christ."

2 Cor. 6:4-6: "Approving ourselves as the ministers of God . . . *in watchings, in fastings.*"

Gal. 4:19: "My little children, of whom *I travail in birth again* until Christ be formed in you."

Eph. 1:16: "*[I] cease not* to give thanks for you, making mention of you *in my prayers.*"

Eph. 3:14-16: "*I bow my knees* unto the Father . . . that he would grant you . . . to be strengthened with might by his Spirit in the inner man."

Phil. 1:3, 4, 8, 9: "I thank my God *upon every remembrance of you, always in every prayer of mine* . . . making request with joy. For God is my record, how greatly I long after you all in the bowels of Jesus Christ. And this *I pray.* . . .''

Col. 1:3, 9: "We give thanks to God . . . *praying always for you.* For this cause also, since the day we heard it, *do not cease to pray for you,* and to desire. . . .''

Col. 2:1: "I would that ye knew what *great conflict* I have for you . . . and for as many as have not seen my face in the flesh."

1 Thess. 1:2: "We give thanks to God *always* for all, making mention of you *in our prayers.*"

1 Thess. 3:9, 10: "We joy for your sakes before our God; *night and day praying exceedingly* that we might . . . perfect that which is lacking in your faith."

2 Thess. 1:3, 11: "We are bound to thank God *always* for you. Wherefore also *we pray always* for you."

2 Tim. 1:3: "I thank God . . . that *without ceasing* I have remembrance of thee . . . night and day."

Philemon 4: "I thank my God, making mention of thee *always in my prayers.*"

These passages taken together give us the picture of a man whose words, "Pray without ceasing," were simply the expression of his daily life. He had a great sense of the insufficiency of simple conversion and of the need of the grace and the power of heaven being brought down for the young converts in prayer. He saw the need of much and unceasing prayer, day and night, to bring it down, and was so sure that prayer would bring it down that his life was continual and specific prayer.

Paul had such a sense that everything must come from above, and such a faith that it would come in answer to prayer, that prayer was neither a duty nor a burden. It was the natural turning of the heart to the only place from where it could possibly obtain what it sought for others.

The Contents of Paul's Prayers

It is just as important to know *what* Paul prayed as to know how frequently and earnestly he did so. Intercession is a spiritual work. Our confidence in it will depend much on our knowing that we ask according to the will of God. The more distinctly we ask heavenly things, which we feel at once God alone can bestow and which we are sure He will bestow, the more direct and urgent will our appeal be to God alone. The more impossible the things are that we seek, the more we will turn from all human work to prayer and to God alone.

In the Epistles, in addition to expressions in which he speaks of his praying, we have a number of distinct prayers in which Paul expresses his heart's desire for those to whom he writes. In these we see that his first desire was always that they might be established in the Christian life. Much as he praised God when he heard of conversion, he knew how feeble the young converts were. He knew nothing would avail for their establishment without the grace of the Spirit prayed down. If we notice some of the main points of these prayers, we shall see what he asked and obtained.

Consider the two prayers in Ephesians—the one for light, the other for strength. In the former (1:15-23), he prays for the Spirit of wisdom to enlighten them to know their calling, their inheritance, and the mighty power of God working in them. Spiritual enlightenment and knowledge was their great need, to be obtained for them by prayer.

In the latter (3:14-19), he asks that the power they had been led to see in Christ might work in them. He asks that they be strengthened with divine might, so as to have the indwelling Christ, the love that surpasses knowledge, and the fullness of God actually come on them. These were things that could only come direct from heaven; these were things he asked and expected. If we want to learn Paul's art of intercession, we must ask nothing less for believers in our days.

Look at the prayer in Philippians (1:9-11). There, too, it is first for spiritual knowledge, then a blameless life, and then a fruitful life to the glory of God. This is also true in the beautiful prayer in Colossians (1:9-11)—first, spiritual knowledge and understanding of God's will, then the strengthening with all might to all patience and joy.

Consider the two prayers in 1 Thess. 3:12, 13 and 5:23. The one: "The Lord make you to increase and abound in love one toward another . . . [that] he may stablish your *hearts unblameable in holiness.*" The other: "God . . . *sanctify you wholly;* and your whole spirit and soul and body be preserved blameless." The very words are so high that we hardly understand, much less believe and even less experience what they mean. Paul so lived in

the heavenly world, and was so at home in the holiness and omnipotence of God and His love, that such prayers were the natural expression of what he knew God could and would do.

"God stablish your hearts unblameable in holiness"; "God
sanctify you wholly." The man who believes in these things and
desires them will pray for them for others. The prayers are all a
proof that he seeks for them the very life of heaven upon earth. No
wonder that he is not tempted to trust in any human means, but
looks for it from heaven alone. Again, I say, the more we take
Paul's prayers as our pattern, and make his desires our own for
believers for whom we pray, the more will prayer to the God of
heaven become as our daily breath.

Paul's Requests for Prayer

Paul's requests are no less instructive than his own prayers for
the saints. They prove that he does not count prayer a special
prerogative of an apostle; he calls the humblest and simplest believer to claim his right. They prove that he does not think that
only the new converts or feeble Christians need prayer; he himself is, as a member of the body, dependent upon his brethren
and their prayers.

After Paul had preached the gospel for twenty years, he still
asks for prayer that he may speak as he ought to speak. Not once
for all, not for a time, but day by day and without ceasing, grace
must be sought and brought down from heaven for his work.
United, continued waiting on God is to Paul the only hope of the
Church. When the Holy Spirit came, a heavenly life, the life of
the Lord in heaven, entered the world; nothing but unbroken
communication with heaven can maintain it.

Listen how Paul asks for prayer, and with what urgency—
Rom. 15:30: "*I beseech you*, brethren, for the Lord Jesus Christ's
sake, and for the love of the Spirit, that ye *strive together with
me in your prayers* to God for me; that I may be delivered from
them that do not believe in Judaea; and . . . that I may come
unto you with joy by the will of God." How remarkably both
prayers were answered: The Roman world-power, which in Pilate
with Christ, and in Herod with Peter at Philippi, had proved its
antagonism to God's kingdom, suddenly becomes Paul's protec-
tor and secures him a safe convoy to Rome. This can only be

accounted for by these prayers.

Consider these other requests by Paul:

2 Cor. 1:10, 11: "In whom we trust that he will yet deliver us; *ye also helping together by prayer* for us."

Eph. 6:18-20: "Praying always with all prayer and supplication in the Spirit . . . for all saints; *and for me*, that . . . I may open my mouth boldly . . . that herein I may speak boldly, as I ought to speak."

Phil. 1:19: "I know that this [trouble] shall turn to my salvation through your prayer, and the supply of the Spirit of Jesus Christ."

Col. 4:2-4: "Continue in prayer . . . withal praying also *for us*, that God would open unto us a door of utterance, to speak the mystery of Christ . . . that I may make it manifest, as I ought to speak."

1 Thess. 5:25: "Brethren, pray for us."

Philemon 22: "I trust that through your prayers I shall be given unto you."

We saw how Christ prayed, and taught His disciples to pray. We see how Paul prayed, and taught the churches to pray. As the Master called, so the servant calls us to believe and to prove that prayer is the power both of the ministry and of the Church.

Paul's faith is summarized in these remarkable words concerning a situation that caused him grief: "This shall turn to my salvation through your prayer, and the supply of the Spirit of Jesus Christ." He depended upon his Lord in heaven and equally upon his brethren on earth, to secure the supply of that Spirit for him. The Spirit from heaven and prayer on earth were to Paul, as to the twelve after Pentecost, inseparably linked. We speak often of apostolic zeal and devotion and power. May God give us a revival of apostolic *prayer*.

Does the work of intercession take the place in the Church it ought to have? Is it commonly understood in the Lord's work that everything depends upon getting from God that "supply of the Spirit of Christ" for and in ourselves that can give our work its real power to bless? This is Christ's divine order for all work—His own and that of His servants. This is the pattern Paul followed: first come every day, as having nothing, and receive from God "the supply of the Spirit" in intercession. Then go and impart what has come to you from heaven.

In all His instructions, our Lord Jesus spoke more frequently to His disciples about their praying than their preaching. In the farewell discourse, He said little about preaching, but much about the Holy Spirit, and about their asking whatsoever they would in His name.

If we are to return to this life of the first apostles and of Paul, we must genuinely accept the truth daily that *my first work, my only strength is intercession*—to secure the power of God on the souls entrusted to me. We must first have the courage to confess past sin, and to believe that there is deliverance. Breaking old habits, resisting the clamor of pressing duties that have always had priority, making every other call subordinate to this one— whether others approve or not—will not be easy at first. But the men or women who are faithful will not only have a reward themselves, but become benefactors to their brethren. "Thou shalt be called, The repairer of the breach, The restorer of paths to dwell in."

But is it really possible that those who have never been able to face or much less overcome the difficulty, can still become mighty in prayer? Tell me, was it really possible for Jacob to become Israel—a prince who prevailed with God? It was. The things that are impossible with men are possible with God. Have you not actually received from the Father, as the great fruit of Christ's redemption, the Spirit of supplication, the Spirit of intercession? Just pause and think what that means. Will you still doubt whether God is able to make you "strivers with God," princes who prevail with Him?

We must banish all fear, and in faith claim the grace for which we have the Holy Spirit dwelling in us—the grace of supplication, the grace of intercession. We must quietly, perseveringly believe that He lives in us, and will enable us to do our work. We must in faith not fear to accept and yield to the great truth that intercession, as it is the great work of the King on the throne, *is the great work of His servants on earth.*

We have the Holy Spirit, who brings the Christ-life into our hearts, to ready us for this work. Let us at once begin and stir up the gift within us. As we set aside each day our time for intercession, and count upon the Spirit's enabling power, the confidence will grow that we can, in our measure, follow Paul even as he followed Christ.

CHAPTER FOURTEEN

God Seeks Intercessors

"I have set watchmen upon thy walls, O Jerusalem, which shall never hold their peace day nor night: ye that make mention of the Lord [are the Lord's remembrancers], keep not silence, and give him no rest . . . till he make Jerusalem a praise in the earth" (Isa. 62:6, 7).

"And he saw that there was *no man*, and wondered that there was *no intercessor*" (Isa. 59:16).

"And I looked, and there was *none to help*; and I wondered, and there was *none to uphold*" (Isa. 63:5).

"There is *none* that calleth upon thy name, that stirreth himself to take hold of thee" (Isa. 64:7).

"And I sought for a man . . . that should stand in the gap before me for the land, that I should not destroy it; but *I found none*" (Ezek. 22:30).

"I chose you, and appointed you, that ye should go and bear fruit: that whatsoever ye shall ask of the Father in my name, he may give it you" (John 15:16).

In the study of the starry heavens, much depends upon a clear understanding of relative sizes or magnitudes. Without some sense of the size of the heavenly bodies, that appear so small to the eye, and yet are so great, and of the almost infinite extent of the regions in which they move, though they appear so near and so familiar, there can be no true knowledge of the heavenly world or its relation to this earth. It is even so with the spiritual heavens and the heavenly life in which we are called to live. It is especially so in the life of intercession, that wonderful interaction between heaven and earth. Everything depends upon the right understanding of magnitudes or relative importance in the spiritual realm.

Think of the three that come first: There is a world, with its needs entirely dependent on and waiting to be helped by intercession; there is a God in heaven, with His all-sufficient supply for all those needs, waiting to be asked; there is a Church, with its magnificent calling and its sure promises, waiting to be roused to a sense of its awesome responsibility and power.

God seeks intercessors. There is a world with perishing millions. Intercession is its only hope. Much of love and work is comparatively vain because there is so little intercession. Billions live as if there never had been a Son of God to die for them. Millions every year pass into the outer darkness without hope. Of the millions bearing the Christian name the great majority live in utter ignorance or indifference.

Millions of feeble, sickly Christians, thousands of wearied workers who could be blessed by intercession, could help themselves to become mighty in intercession. Churches and missions sacrifice life and labor often with little result for lack of intercession. Souls, each one worth more than worlds, are worth nothing less than the price paid for them in Christ's blood. They are within reach of the power that can be won by intercession. We surely have no conception of the magnitude of the work to be done by God's intercessors, or we should cry to God above everything to give from heaven the spirit of intercession.

God seeks intercessors. There is a God of glory able to meet all these needs. We are told that He delights in mercy, that He waits to be gracious, that He longs to pour out His blessing. The love that gave the Son to death is the measure of the love that each moment hovers over every human being. But still He does not help. And there they perish, millions each year in China alone. It is as if God does not move.

If God does so love and long to bless, there must be some inscrutable reason for His holding back. What can it be? Scripture says, "Because of your unbelief." It is the faithlessness and consequent unfaithfulness of God's people. He has taken them into partnership with himself; He has honored them and bound himself, by making their prayers a standard against which to measure the working of His power.

Lack of intercession is one of the chief causes of lack of blessing. Oh, that we would turn eye and heart from everything else and fix them upon this God who hears prayer until the magnificence of His promises and His power and His purpose of love overwhelmed us! How our whole life and heart would be transformed into intercession.

God seeks intercessors. There is a third magnitude to which our eyes must be opened, the stupendous privilege and power of the intercessors. There is a false humility, which makes a great virtue of self-depreciation—because it has never seen its utter nothingness. If it realized that, it would never apologize for its feebleness, but glory in its utter weakness, as the one condition of Christ's power resting on it. It would judge of itself, its power and influence before God in prayer, as little by what it sees or feels, as we judge the size of the sun or stars by what the eye can see.

Faith sees man created, in God's image and likeness, to be God's representative in this world and have dominion over it. Faith sees man redeemed and lifted into union with Christ, abiding in Him, identified with Him, and clothed with His power in intercession. Faith sees the Holy Spirit dwelling and praying in the heart and through our sighings, making intercession according to God. Faith sees the intercession of the saints as a part of the life of the Holy Trinity, the believer as God's child asking of the Father, in the Son, through the Spirit. Faith sees something of the divine fitness and beauty of this scheme of salvation through intercession and wakens the soul to an awareness of its amazing and wonderful destiny. Then faith girds the soul with strength for the call to the blessed sacrifice of self.

God seeks intercessors. When God called His people out of Egypt, He separated the priestly tribe, to draw near to Him, and stand before Him, and bless the people in His name. From time to time He sought, found and honored intercessors, for whose sake He spared or blessed His people. When our Lord left the earth, He said to the inner circle He had gathered around Him, which was an inner circle with a special devotion to His service, and to which access is still free to every disciple: "I chose you, and ordained you . . . that whatsoever ye shall ask of the Father in my name, he may give it you."

We have already noticed that three wonderful words— *whatsoever in my name, it shall be done*—were repeated six times. In them Christ placed the powers of the heavenly world at the disciples' disposal—not for their own selfish use but in the interests of His kingdom. How wonderfully they used this power we know. Down through the ages since that time, apostles have had their successors, men who have proved how surely God works in answer to prayer.

We may praise God that, in our days too, there is an ever-increasing number who begin to see and prove that in church and mission, in large societies and little circles and individual effort, intercession is the chief thing, the power that moves God and opens heaven. They are learning, and long to learn better. They desire that all may learn, that in all work for souls intercession must take the first place. Those who in the power of the Holy Spirit have received from heaven what they are to communicate to others will be best able to do the Lord's work.

God seeks intercessors. God had His appointed servants in Israel—watchmen He appointed to cry to Him day and night and give Him no rest. Yet He often had to wonder and complain that there was no intercessor, none to stir himself up to take hold of God's strength.

In our day He still waits and wonders that there are not more intercessors, that all His children do not give themselves to this highest and holiest work. He is surprised that the many who do so, do not engage in it more intensely and perseveringly. He wonders at ministers of His gospel complaining that their duties do not allow them to find time for this, which He considers their first, their highest, their most delightful, their alone effective work. He wonders at His sons and daughters, who have forsaken home and friends for His sake and the gospel's, falling so short in what He meant to be their abiding strength—the receiving daily all they needed to impart to the dark heathen. He wonders at the multitudes of His children who have hardly any conception of what intercession is. He wonders at the multitudes more who have learned that it is their duty, and seek to obey it, but confess that they know but little of the actual laying hold upon God or prevailing with Him.

God seeks intercessors. God longs to dispense larger blessings. He longs to reveal His power and glory as God and to show His saving love more abundantly. He seeks intercessors in larger number, and greater power to prepare the way of the Lord. He seeks them. Where could He seek them except in His Church? And how does He expect to find them? He entrusted to His Church the task of telling of their Lord's need, the task of encouraging and training and preparing them for His holy service. And He ever returns seeking fruit, seeking intercessors.

In His Word God has spoken of the "widow indeed . . . [who] trusts in God, and continueth in supplication . . . night and day." He looks to see if the Church is training the great army of aged men and women, whose time of outward work is past, but who can strengthen the army of the "elect, who cry to him day and night."

God looks to the great host of young people who have given themselves away in a solemn pledge to obey the Lord Jesus Christ at all cost, and wonders how many are being trained to pass beyond the brightness of the weekly prayer meeting and its confession of loyalty to swell the army of secret intercessors that is to save souls.

God looks to the thousands of young men and young women in training for the work of ministry and mission, and gazes longingly to see if the Church is teaching them that intercession—power with God—must be their first responsibility.

God looks to see whether ministers and missionaries are understanding their opportunity and training the believers of their congregation into those who can "help together" by their prayer, and can "strive with them in their prayers." As Christ seeks the lost sheep until He finds it, God seeks intercessors (Appendix 6).

God seeks intercessors. He will not, He cannot, take the work out of the hands of His Church. Therefore He comes, calling and pleading in many ways. Perhaps by a man whom He raises up to live a life of faith in His service and to prove how actually and abundantly He answers prayer; then another time by the story of a church which makes prayer for souls its starting point, and bears testimony to God's faithfulness; sometimes in a mission which proves how special prayer can meet special need and bring down the power of the Spirit; sometimes again by a season of revival coming in answer to united urgent supplication. In these and many other ways God is showing us what intercession can do. He beseeches us to wake up and train His great host to be, every one, a people of intercessors.

God seeks intercessors. God sends His servants out to call them. Let ministers make this a part of their duty. Let them make their church a training school of intercession. Give the people definite objects for prayer. Encourage them to take a definite time for it even if it be only ten minutes every day. Help them to understand the boldness they may use with God. Teach them to expect and look for answers. Show them what it is first to pray and get an answer in secret, and then carry the answer and impart and scatter the blessing to others. Tell everyone who is master of his own time that he is as the angels, free to wait before the throne and then to go out and minister to the heirs of salvation. Sound out the blessed tidings that this honor is for all of God's people. There is no difference. That servant girl, this day laborer, that bedridden invalid, this daughter in her mother's home, these men and young men in business—all are called and all are needed. God seeks intercessors.

God seeks intercessors. As ministers take up the work of finding and training intercessors, it will challenge the ministers themselves to pray more. Christ gave Paul to be a pattern of His grace before He made him a preacher of it. It has been well said, "The first duty of a clergyman is humbly to pray that all he would have God do in his people may be first truly and fully done in himself."

The effort to bring this message of God may cause much heart searching and humiliation. All the better. The best practice in doing a thing is helping others to do it.

O servants of Christ, set as watchmen to cry to God day and night, let us awake to our holy calling. Let us believe in the power of intercession. Let us practice it. Let us seek on behalf of our people to get from God himself the Spirit and the life we preach. With our spirit and life given up to God in intercession, the Spirit and life that God gives them through us cannot fail to be the life of intercession too.

CHAPTER FIFTEEN

The Coming Revival

"Wilt thou not revive us again: that thy people may rejoice in thee?" (Ps. 85:6).

"O Lord, revive thy work in the midst of the years" (Hab. 3:2).

"Though I walk in the midst of trouble, thou wilt revive me . . . thy right hand shall save me" (Ps. 38:7).

"I dwell . . . with him that is of a contrite and humble spirit to revive the spirit of the humble, and to renew the heart of the contrite ones" (Isa. 57:15).

"Come, and let us return unto the Lord: for he hath torn, and he will heal us. . . . He will revive us" (Hos. 6:1, 2).

"The coming revival"—one frequently hears the word. There are many teachers who see the signs of its approach, and confidently herald its speedy appearance. The increase of interest in missions, the news of revivals in places where all were dead or cold; the hosts of our young people gathered together in Christian youth groups; the open doors everywhere in the Christian and the heathen world; the victories already won in the fields white unto the harvest, wherever believing, hopeful workers enter—all strengthen the assurance of a coming time of power and blessing such as we have not known. The Church is about to enter on a new era of increasing spirituality and greater extension.

There are others who, while admitting the truth of some of these facts, still fear that the conclusions drawn from them are one-sided and premature. They see the interest in missions increased, but point at the small circle to which it is confined, and how utterly out of proportion it is to what it ought to be.

To the great majority of Church members and to the greater part of the Church, the issue is as yet anything but a vital question. They remind us of the power of worldliness and formality, of the increase of the money-making and pleasure-loving spirit

108

among professing Christians, of the lack of spirituality in so many of our churches, and the continuing and apparently increasing estrangement of multitudes from God's Day and Word as proof that the great revival has certainly not begun, and is hardly thought of by the most. They say that they do not see the deep humiliation, the intense desire, the fervent prayer which appear as the forerunners of every true revival.

There are right-hand and left-hand errors which are equally dangerous. We must seek as much to be kept from the superficial optimism, which never is able to gauge the extent of evil, as from the hopeless pessimism, which can neither praise God for what He has done nor trust Him for what He is ready to do. The former will lose itself in a happy congratulation of self that rejoices in its zeal and diligence and apparent success. It never sees the need of confession and great striving in prayer needed before we are prepared to meet and conquer the hosts of darkness. The latter virtually gives over the world to Satan, and almost prays and rejoices to see things get worse, to hasten the coming of Him who is to put all right.

May God keep us from either error, and fulfill the promise, "Thine ears shall hear a word behind thee, saying, This is the way, walk ye in it, when ye turn to the right hand, and when ye turn to the left." Let us listen to the lessons suggested by the passages we have quoted; they may help us to pray the prayer aright: "Revive thy work, O Lord!"

1. *"Revive thy work, O Lord!"* Read again this chapter's scripture texts. See how they all contain the one thought: Revival is God's work, He alone can give it, it must come from above. We are frequently in danger of looking to what God has done and is doing, and to count on that as the pledge that He will at once do more. Yet He may be blessing us up to the measure of our faith or self-sacrifice, and cannot give larger measure until there has been a new discovery and confession of what is hindering Him. We also may be looking to all the signs of life and good around us, and congratulating ourselves on all the organizations and agencies that are being created, while the need of God's mighty and direct interposition is not rightly felt, and the entire dependence upon Him not cultivated.

Regeneration, the giving of divine life, we all acknowledge to be God's act, a miracle of His power. The restoring or reviving of the divine life in a soul or a Church is equally a supernatural work. To have the spiritual discernment that can understand the signs of the heavens, and foretell the coming revival, we need to enter deep into God's mind and will as to its conditions, and the preparedness of those who pray for it or are to be used to bring it about. "Surely the Lord God will do nothing, but he revealeth his secret unto his servants the prophets." It is God who is to give the revival; it is God who reveals His secret; it is the spirit of absolute dependence upon God, giving Him the honor and the glory, that will prepare for it.

2. *"Revive thy work, O Lord!"* A second lesson suggested is that the revival God is to give will be given in answer to prayer. It must be asked and received directly from God himself.

Those who know anything of the history of revivals will remember how often this has been proved—both larger and more local revivals have been distinctly traced to special prayer. In our own day there are numbers of congregations and missions where special or permanent revivals are—all glory be to God—connected with systematic, believing prayer. The coming revival will be no exception. An extraordinary spirit of prayer, urging believers to much secret and united prayer, pressing them to "labor fervently" in their supplications, will be one of the surest signs of approaching showers and floods of blessing.

Let all who are burdened with the lack of spirituality, with the low state of the life of God in believers, listen to the call that comes to all. If there is to be revival—a mighty, divine revival—it will need, on our part, corresponding wholeheartedness in prayer and faith.

Let not one believer think himself too weak to help, or imagine that he will not be missed. If he will only begin, the gift that is in him may be so stirred that, for his circle or neighborhood, he shall be God's chosen intercessor.

Think of the need of souls, of all the sins and failings among God's people, of the little power there is in so much of the preaching. Then begin to cry every day, "Wilt thou not revive us again: that thy people may rejoice in thee?" Let us have the truth graven deep in our hearts: Every revival comes, as Pentecost came, as the fruit of united and continued prayer. The coming revival must begin with a great revival of prayer. It is in the closet, with the door shut, that the sound of abundance of rain will be first heard. An increase of secret prayer with ministers and members will be the sure indication of blessing.

3. *"Revive thy work, O Lord!"* A third lesson our texts teach is that the revival is promised to the humble and contrite. We want the revival to come upon the proud and the self-satisfied, to break them down and save them. God will give this, but only on the condition that those who see and feel the sin of others take their burden of confession and bear it.

All those who pray for and claim in faith God's reviving power for His Church must humble themselves with the confession of its sins. Need of revival always points to previous decline, and decline was always caused by sin. Humiliation and contrition have always been the conditions for revival. In all intercession confession of man's sin and God's righteous judgment is an essential element.

Throughout the history of Israel we continually see this. It is demonstrated in the reformations under the pious kings of Judah. We hear it in the prayers of men like Ezra, Nehemiah, and Daniel. In Isaiah, Jeremiah, and Ezekiel, as well as in the minor prophets, it is the keynote of all the warning as well as all the promise. If there be no humiliation and forsaking of sin, there can be no revival or deliverance. "These men have set up their idols in their heart. . . , Should I be inquired of at all by them?" "To this man will I look, even to him that is poor and of a contrite spirit, and trembleth at my word." Amid the most gracious promises of divine visitation there is ever this note: "Be ashamed and confounded for your own ways, O House of Israel."

We find the same emphasis in the New Testament. The Sermon on the Mount promises the kingdom to the poor and them that mourn. In the Epistles to the Corinthians and Galatians the religion of man, of worldly wisdom and confidence in the flesh, is exposed and denounced; without its being confessed and forsaken, all the promises of grace and the Spirit will be vain.

The epistles to the seven churches show us five churches of which God, out of whose mouth goes the sharp, two-edged sword, says that He has something against them. In each of these the keyword of His message is—not to the unconverted, but to the

Church—*Repent*. All the glorious promises which each of these epistles contain share one condition, right down to the invitation to "Open the door, I will come in" and the promise, "He that overcometh will . . . sit with me on my throne," all are dependent on that one word—*repent*!

If there is to be a revival—not among the unsaved but in our churches, to give a holy, spiritual membership—will not that trumpet sound need to be heard—*Repent*! Was it only in Israel, in the ministry of kings and prophets, that there was so much evil in God's people to be cleansed away? Was it only in the Church of the first century that Paul and James and our Lord himself had to speak such sharp words?

Is there not in the Church of our days an idolatry of money and talent and culture—a worldly spirit—making it unfaithful to its one Husband and Lord, a confidence in the flesh which grieves and resists God's Holy Spirit? Is there not almost everywhere a confession of the lack of spirituality and spiritual power?

Let all who long for the coming revival, and seek to hasten it by their prayers, pray this above everything, that the Lord may prepare His prophets to go before Him at His bidding: "Cry aloud, spare not, lift up thy voice like a trumpet, and shew my people their transgression."

Every deep revival among God's people must have its roots in a deep sense and confession of sin. Until those who would lead the Church in the path of revival bear faithful testimony against the sins of the Church, it is to be feared that it will find people unprepared. Men would prefer to have a revival as the outgrowth of their agencies and progress. God's way is the opposite. Out of death, acknowledged as the reward of sin, confessed as utter helplessness, God revives. He revives the heart of the contrite one.

4. *"Revive thy work, O Lord!"* There is a final thought, suggested by the text from Hosea. It is as we return *to the Lord* that revival will come; for if we had not wandered from Him, His life would be among us in power. "Come and let us return to the Lord: for he hath torn, and he will heal us; he hath smitten, and he will bind us up. . . . He will raise us up, and we shall live in his sight."

As we have said, where there is no sense or confession of

wandering, there can be no return to the Lord. *Let us return to the Lord* must be the keynote of the revival. Let us return, acknowledging and forsaking whatever there has been in the Church that is not entirely according to His mind and spirit. Let us return and yield up and cast out whatever there has been in our religion of the power of God's two great enemies—confidence in the flesh or the spirit of the world. In the acknowledgement of how undividedly God must have us, to fill us with His Spirit, and use us for the kingdom of His Son, let us return. Return in the surrender of a dependence and a devotion which has no measure but the absolute claim of Him who is the Lord! With our whole heart, let us come back, asking that He may make and keep us wholly His. He will revive us, and we shall live in His sight. Let us turn to the God of Pentecost, as Christ led His disciples to turn to Him, and the God of Pentecost will turn to us.

It is for this returning to the Lord that the great work of intercession is needed. Here the coming revival must find its strength. Let us begin as individuals to plead in secret with God, confessing whatever we see of sin or hindrance in ourselves or others. If there were not one other sin, surely in the lack of prayer there is reason enough for repentance and confession and returning to the Lord.

Let us seek to foster the spirit of confession and supplication and intercession in those around us; help to encourage and to train those who think themselves too weak; lift up our voice to proclaim the great truths. The revival must come from above. The revival must be received in faith from above but brought down by prayer. The revival comes to the humble and contrite, for them to carry to others.

If we return to the Lord with our whole heart, He will revive us. On those who see these truths rests the solemn responsibility of yielding themselves to share and carry out these things.

As each of us pleads for revival throughout the Church, let us also cry to God for our own neighborhood or sphere of work. Let there be "great searchings of heart" in every minister and worker as to whether they are ready to give such time and strength to prayer as God would have. Just as in public they are leaders of their larger or smaller circles, let them in secret take their places in the front rank of the great intercession host. They must prevail with God before the great revival and the floods of blessing can come. Of all who speak, think, or long for revival, let not one hold back in this great work of honest, earnest, definite pleading: Revive thy work, O Lord! Wilt thou not revive us again?

Come and return to the Lord. He will revive us! Let us follow on to know the Lord. "*His going forth* is prepared as the morning; and *he shall come unto us* as the rain, as the latter and former rain unto the earth." Amen. So be it.

APPENDICES

Appendix 1

Just this day I have been counseling a very earnest lady missionary from India. She confesses and mourns the lack of prayer. But—in India at least—it can hardly be otherwise, she insists. You have only the morning hours, from six to eleven, for your work. Some have attempted to rise at four and get the time they think they need but have suffered and had to give it up. Some have tried to take time after lunch and been found asleep on their knees. You are not your own master, and must act with others. No one who has not been in India can understand the difficulty; sufficient time for much intercession cannot be secured.

Were it only in the heat of India the difficulty existed, one might be silent. But, alas, in the coldest winter in London, and in the moderate climate of South Africa, there is the same trouble everywhere. If once we really felt that *intercession is the most important part of our work* and that the securing of God's presence and power in full measure is the essential thing—our first duty—our hours of work would all be made subordinate to this one thing.

May God show us all whether there is an insurmountable difficulty for which we are responsible, whether it be only a mistake we are making or a sin by which we are grieving Him and hindering His Spirit!

If we ask the question George Muller once asked of a Christian, who complained that he could not find time sufficient for the study of the Word and prayer, whether an hour less work, leaving four hours, with the soul dwelling in the full light of God, would not be more prosperous and effective than five hours with the depressing consciousness of unfaithfulness, and the loss of the power that could be obtained in prayer, the answer will not be difficult. The more we think of it, the more we feel that when earnest, godly workers allow, against their better will, the spiritual to be crowded out by incessant occupation and the fatigue it brings, it must be because the spiritual life is not sufficiently strong in them to make the lesser things wait till the presence of God in Christ and the power of the Spirit have been fully secured.

Listen to Christ saying, *"Render unto Caesar the things that are Caesar's"*—let duty and work have their place—"and unto God the things that are God's." Let the worship in the Spirit, the entire dependence and continued waiting upon God for the full experience of His presence and power every day, and the strength of Christ working in us, ever have the first place. The whole question is simply this: Is God to have the place, the love, the trust, the time for personal fellowship He claims so that all our working shall be God working in us?

Appendix 2

Let me tell here a story that occurs in one of Dr. Boardman's works. He had been invited by a lady of good position, well known as a successful worker among her husband's dependents, to come and address them. "And then," she added, "I want to speak to you about a bit of bondage of my own." After he had addressed her meeting, and found many brought to Christ through her, he wondered what her trouble might be. She soon told him.

God had blessed her work, but she was sorry to say the enjoymnet she once had had in God's Word and secret prayer had been lost. She had tried her utmost to get it back and had failed.

"Ah! that is just your mistake," he said.

"How is that? Ought I not to do my best to have the coldness removed?"

"Tell me," he said, "were you saved by doing your best?"

"Oh, no! I tried long to do that, but only found rest when I ceased trying, and trusted Christ."

"That is what you need to do now. Enter your closet at the appointed time, however dull you feel, and place yourself before your Lord. Do not try to rouse an earnestness you do not feel. Quietly say to Him that He sees how all is wrong, how helpless you are. Then trust Him to bless you. He will do it. As you trust quietly, His Spirit will work."

The simple story may teach many a Christian a most blessed lesson in the life of prayer. You have accepted Christ Jesus' offer to make you whole, and give you strength to walk in newness of life; you have claimed the Holy Spirit to be in you the Spirit of supplication and intercession; but do not wonder if your feelings are not all at once changed, or if your power of prayer does not come in the way you would like. It is a life of faith. By faith we receive the Holy Spirit and all His workings. Faith regards neither sight nor feeling, but rests, even when there appears to be no power to pray, in the assurance that the Spirit is praying in us as we bow quietly before God.

He that thus waits in faith, and honors the Holy Spirit, and yields himself to Him, will soon find that prayer will begin to come. And he that perseveres in the faith that through Christ and by the Spirit each prayer, however feeble, is acceptable to God, will learn the lesson that it is possible to be taught by the Spirit and led to walk worthy of the Lord to all well pleasing.

Appendix 3

Just yesterday again, three days after the conversation mentioned in the previous note, I met a devoted young missionary lady from the interior. During a conversation on prayer she remarked, "But it is really impossible to find the time to pray as we wish to."

I could only answer, "Time is a quantity that accommodates itself to our will; what our hearts really consider of *first importance,* in the day, we will soon succeed in finding time for."

It must surely be that the ministry of intercession has never been put before our students in theological training as the most important part of their life work. We have thought of our work in preaching or visiting as our real duty, and of prayer as a subordinate means to do this work successfully. Would not the whole position be changed if we regarded the ministry of intercession as the chief thing—*getting the blessing and power of God* for the soul entrusted to us? Then our work would take its right place, and become the subordinate one of dispensing blessings which we had received from God.

It was when the friend at midnight, in answer to his prayer, had received from another as much as he needed that he could supply his hungry friend. It was the intercession, going out and importuning, that was the difficult work; returning home with his rich supply to impart was easy, joyful work. This is Christ's divine order for all our work: First come, in utter poverty every day, and get from God the blessing in intercession. Go then with joy to impart it.

Appendix 4

Let me repeat, no book has so helped me with an insight into the place and work of the Holy Spirit in redemption as William Law's *Power of the Spirit.**

He says that God's one object was to dwell in man, making him partaker of His goodness and glory. This way of God himself living and working in man gives one the key to what Pentecost and the sending forth of the Spirit of God's Son into our hearts really means. It is Christ in God's name regaining and retaking possession of the home He had created for himself. It is God entering into the secret depths of our nature there to "work to will and to do," to work "that which is well-pleasing in his sight through Christ Jesus."

As this truth enters into us, we see that there is and can be no good in us except what God works. We then see light on the divine mystery of prayer, and believe in the Holy Spirit as breathing within us desires which God will fulfill when we yield to them, and in faith present them in the name of Christ.

Equally as wonderful and prevailing as the intercession and prayer passing from the incarnate Son to the Father in heaven is our relationship with God. When the Spirit, who is God, breathes and prays in us amid all our feebleness His heaven-born divine petitions, what a heavenly thing prayer becomes.

The latter part of Law's book consists of extracts of his letters. No one who will take the time to read and master the simple but deep teaching they contain can help being wonderfully strengthened in the confidence which is needed if we are to pray much and boldly. As we learn that the Holy Spirit is within us to reveal Christ and to make us partakers of His death, His life, His merit, His disposition, so that He is formed within us, we will begin to see how divinely right and sure it is that our intercessions in His name must be heard. His own Spirit maintains the living union with himself, in whom we are brought near to God, and gives us boldness of access. What I have so feebly said in the chapter on the Spirit of supplication will get new meaning; and the exercise of prayer a new attractiveness. Its solemn divine mystery will humble us, its unspeakable privilege lift us up in faith and adoration.

---

*Ed. by Andrew Murray, published by Bethany House Publishers.

Appendix 5

There is a question, the deepest of all, on which I have not entered in this book. I have spoken of the lack of prayer in the individual Christian as a symptom of a disease. But what shall we say of it, that there is such a widespread failure to give a due proportion of time and strength to prayer? Do we not need to ask, "How is it that the Church of Christ, endued with the Holy Ghost, cannot train its ministers and workers and members to place first what is first? How is the confession of too little prayer, and the call for more prayer, so frequently heard, and yet the evil continues?"

The Spirit of God, the Spirit of supplication and intercession, *is* in the Church and in every believer. There must surely be some other spirit of great power resisting and hindering this Spirit of God. It is indeed so. The spirit of the world, which under all its beautiful and even religious activities is the spirit of the god of this world, is the great hindrance. Everything that is done on earth, whether within or without the Church, is done by either of these two spirits.

What is in the individual as the flesh is in mankind as the spirit of the world. All the power the flesh has in the individual is due to the place given to the spirit of this world in the Church and in Christian life. The spirit of the world is the great hindrance to the Spirit of prayer. All our most earnest calls to men to pray more will be vain unless this evil is acknowledged and combated and overcome. The believer and the Church must be entirely freed from the spirit of the world.

How is this to be done? There is but one way—the Cross of Christ, "by whom," as Paul says, "the world is crucified unto me, and I unto the world." It is only through death to the world that we can be freed from its spirit. The separation must be vital and entire. It is only through the acceptance of our crucifixion with Christ that we can live out this confession, and, as crucified to the world, maintain the position of irreconcilable hostility to whatever is of its spirit and not of the Spirit of God. It is only God himself who, by His divine power, can lead us into and keep us daily dead to sin and alive unto God in Christ Jesus. The cross, with its shame and its separation from the world, and its death to all that is of flesh and of self, is the only power that can conquer the spirit of the world.

I have felt so strongly that the truth needs to be freshly asserted, that I hope, if it please God, to publish a volume, *The Cross of Christ,* with the inquiry into what God's Word teaches as to our actual participation with Christ in His crucifixion. Christ prayed on the way to the cross. He prayed himself to the cross. He prayed on the cross. He prays ever as the fruit of the cross. As the Church lives on the cross, and the cross lives in the Church, the spirit of prayer will be given. In Christ it was the crucifixion spirit and death that was the source of the intercession Spirit and power. With us it can be no other way either.

Appendix 6

I have frequently spoken of the need of training Christians for the work of intercession. In a previous note I have asked the question whether, in the teaching of our theological training, sufficient attention is given to prayer as the most important, and in some ways the most difficult part of the work for which the students are being prepared. I have wondered whether it might not be possible to offer those students who are willing a course of training, with help in the way of hints and suggestions as to what is needed to give prayer the place and the power in our ministry it ought to have.

As a rule, it is in the student life that the character must be formed for future years, and it is in the present student world that the Church of the future must be influenced. If God allows me to carry out a plan that is hardly quite mature yet, I want to publish a volume, *The Student's Prayer Manual*. This would combine the teaching of Scripture as to what is most needed to make men of prayer of us, with such practical directions as may help a young Christian, preparing to devote his life to God's service successfully, to cultivate such a spirit and habit of prayer as shall abide with him through all his coming life and labors.

PRAY WITHOUT CEASING
(A thirty-one-day course)

Helps to Intercession

"Praying always with all prayer and supplication in the Spirit, and watching thereunto with all perseverance and supplication for all saints; and for me. . ." (Eph. 6:18, 19).

"I exhort, therefore, that, first of all, supplications, prayers, intercessions, and giving of thanks, be made for all men; for kings, and for all that are in authority. . . " (1 Tim. 2:12).

"Pray one for another. . ." (James 5:16).

Pray without ceasing. Who can do this? How can one do it who is surrounded by the cares of daily life? How can a mother love her child without ceasing? How can the eyelid without ceasing hold itself ready to protect the eye? How can I breathe and feel and hear without ceasing? Because all these are the functions of a healthy, natural life. And so, if the spiritual life be healthy, under the full power of the Holy Spirit, praying without ceasing will be natural.

Pray without ceasing. Does it refer to continual acts of prayer, in which we are to persevere till we obtain, or to the spirit of prayerfulness that should animate us all the day? It includes both. The example of our Lord Jesus shows us this. We have to enter our closet for special seasons of prayer; we are at times to persevere there in importunate prayer. We are also all the day to walk in God's presence, with the whole heart set upon heavenly things. Without set times of prayer the spirit of prayer will be dull and feeble. Without the continual prayerfulness the set times will not avail.

Pray without ceasing. Does it refer to prayer for ourselves or others? To both. It is because many confine it to themselves that they fail so in practicing it. It is only when the branch gives itself to bear fruit, more fruit, much fruit, that it can live a healthy life, and expect a rich inflow of sap. The death of Christ brought Him to the place of everlasting intercession. Your death with Him to sin and self sets you free from the care of self, and elevates you to the dignity of intercessor—one who can get life and blessing from God for others. Know your calling; begin this your work. Give yourself wholly to it, and soon you will be finding something of this *"praying always"* within you.

Pray without ceasing. How can I learn it? The best way of learning to do a thing—in fact the only way—is to *do it.* Begin by setting apart some time every day, say ten or fifteen minutes, in which you say to God and to yourself that you come to Him now as intercessor for others. Let it be after your morning or evening prayer, or any other time. If you cannot secure the same time every day, be not troubled. Only see that you do it. Christ chose you and appointed you to pray for others.

If at first you do not feel any special urgency or faith or power in your prayers, do not let that hinder you. Quietly tell your Lord Jesus of your feebleness; believe that the Holy Spirit is in you to teach you to pray; be assured that if you begin, God will help you. God cannot help you unless you begin and keep on.

Pray without ceasing. How do I know what to pray for? If once you begin and think of all the needs around you, you will soon find enough. But to help you, this section was written with subjects and hints for prayer for a month. It is meant that we should use it month by month until we know more fully to follow the Spirit's leading, and have learned, if need be, to make our own list of subjects, and can dispense with it. In regard to the use of these helps, a few words may be needed.

1. *How to pray.* You notice for every day two headings: the one "What to Pray"; the other, "How to Pray." If the subjects were only given, one might fall into the routine of mentioning names and things before God, and the work become a burden. The hints under the heading "How to Pray" are meant to remind of the spiritual nature of the work, of the need of divine help. They will encourage faith in the certainty that God, through the Spirit, will give us grace to pray aright, and will also hear our prayer. One does not at once learn to take his place boldly and to dare to believe that he will be heard.

Take a few moments each day to listen to God's voice

reminding you of how certainly even you will be heard, and calling on you to pray in that faith in your Father, to claim and take the blessing you plead for. And let these words about how to pray enter your hearts and occupy your thoughts at other times too. The work of intercession is Christ's great work on earth, entrusted to Him because He gave himself a sacrifice to God for men. The work of intercession is the greatest work a Christian can do. Give yourself a sacrifice to God for men, and the work will become your glory and your joy too.

2. *What to pray.* Scripture calls us to pray for many things: for all saints, for all men, for kings and all rulers, for all who are in adversity, for the sending forth of laborers, for those who labor in the gospel, for all converts, for believers who have fallen into sin, for one another in our own immediate circles. The Church is now so much larger than when the New Testament was written; the number of forms of work and workers is so much greater; the needs of the Church and the world are so much better known that we need to take time and thought to see where prayer is needed, and to what our heart is most drawn out.

The scriptural calls to prayer demand a large heart, taking in all saints, and all men, and all needs. An attempt has been made in these helps to indicate what the chief subjects are that need prayer, and that ought to interest every Christian.

It will be felt difficult by many to pray for such large spheres as are sometimes mentioned. Let it be understood that in each case we may make special intercession for our own circle of interest coming under that heading. And it is hardly necessary to say, that where one subject appears of more special interest or urgency than another, we are free for a time, day after day, to take up that subject. If only time be really given to intercession, and the spirit of believing intercession be cultivated, the object is attained. While, on the one hand, the heart must be enlarged at times to take in all, the more pointed and definite our prayer can be the better. With this view, space is left in which you can write down special petitions you desire to urge before God.

3. *Answers to prayer.* More than one little book has been published in which Christians may keep a register of their petitions, and note when they were answered. Room has been left on every page for this, so that more definite petitions with regard to

individual souls or special spheres of work may be recorded and the answer looked for. When we pray for all saints, or for missions in general, it is difficult to know when or how our prayer is answered, or whether our prayer has had any part in bringing the answer. It is of extreme importance that we should prove that God hears us, and to this end take note of what answers we look for and when they come. On the day of praying for all saints, take the saints in your congregation, or in your prayer meeting, and ask for a revival among them. Take, in connection with missions, some special station or missionary you are interested in, or more than one, and plead for blessing. And expect and look for its coming that you may praise God.

4. *Prayer circles.* There is no desire in publishing this invitation to intercession to add another to the many existing prayer unions or praying bands. The first object is to stir the many Christians who, through ignorance of their calling or unbelief as to their prayer availing much, take very little part in the work of intercession; and then to help those who do pray to some fuller apprehension of the greatness of the work and the need of giving their whole strength to it.

There is a circle of prayer which asks for prayer on the first day of every month for the fuller manifestation of the power of the Holy Spirit throughout the Church. I have given the words of that invitation as subject for the first day, and taken the same thought as keynote all through. The more one thinks of the need and the promise, and the greatness of the obstacles to be overcome in prayer, the more one feels it must become our life work day by day, that to which every other interest is subordinated.

But while not forming a large prayer union, it is suggested that it may be found helpful to have small prayer circles to unite in prayer, either for one month, with some special object introduced daily along with the others, or through a year or longer, with the view of strengthening each other in the grace of intercession. If a minister were to invite some of his neighboring brethren to join for some special requests along with the printed subjects for supplication, or a number of the more earnest members of his congregation to unite in prayer for revival, some might be trained to take their place in the great work of intercession, who now stand idle because "no man hath hired them."

5. *Who is sufficient for these things?* The more we study and try to practice this grace of intercession, the more we become overwhelmed by its greatness and our feebleness. Let every such impression lead us to hear: "My grace is sufficient for thee," and to answer truthfully, "Our sufficiency is of God."

Take courage; it is in the intercession of Christ you are called to take part. The burden and the agony, the triumph and the victory, are all His. Learn from Him, yield to His Spirit in you, to know how to pray. He gave himself a sacrifice to God for men that He might have the right and power of intercession. "He bare the sin of many, and made intercession for the transgressors."

Let your faith rest boldly on His finished work. Let your heart wholly identify itself with Him in His death and His life. Like Him, give yourself to God a sacrifice for men. It is your highest nobility, it is your true and full union with Him; it will be to you, as to Him, your power of intercession.

Come and give your whole heart and life to intercession, and you will know its blessedness and its power. God asks nothing less; the world needs nothing less; Christ asks nothing less; let nothing less be what we offer to God.

DAY ONE

What to Pray—for the power of the Holy Spirit

"That he would grant you . . . to be strengthened with might by his Spirit" (Eph. 3:16).
"Wait for the promise of the Father" (Acts 1:4).

"Pray for the fuller manifestation of the grace and energy of the blessed Spirit of God, in the removal of all that is contrary to God's revealed will, so that we grieve not the Holy Spirit, but that He may work in mightier power in the Church, for the exaltation of Christ and the blessing of souls."

God has one promise to and through His exalted Son. Our Lord has one gift to His Church. The Church has one need. All prayer unites in the one petition—the power of the Holy Spirit. Make it your one prayer.

How to Pray—as a child asks a father

"If a son shall ask bread of any of you that is a father, will he give him a stone? How much more shall your heavenly Father give the Holy Spirit to them that ask him?" (Luke 11:11, 13).

Ask as simply and trustfully as a child asks for bread. You can do this because "God hath sent forth the Spirit of his Son into your heart, crying, 'Abba, Father.' " This Spirit is in you to give you childlike confidence. In the faith of His praying in you, ask for the power of that Holy Spirit everywhere. Mention places or groups where you specially desire it to be seen.

SPECIAL PETITIONS

_____
_____
_____
_____
_____
_____

DAY TWO

What to Pray—for the Spirit of supplication

"The Spirit itself maketh intercession for us" (Rom. 8:26).
"I will pour . . . the spirit of . . . supplications" (Zech. 12:10).

The evangelization of the world depends first of all upon a revival of prayer. Deeper than the need for men—deep down at the bottom of our spiritless life—is the need for the forgotten secret of prevailing, worldwide prayer.

Every child of God has the Holy Spirit in him to pray. God waits to give the Spirit in full measure. Ask for yourself, and all who join, the outpouring of the Spirit of supplication. Ask it for your own prayer circle.

How to Pray—in the Spirit

"Praying always with all prayer and supplication in the Spirit" (Eph. 6:18).
"Praying in the Holy Ghost" (Jude 20).

On His resurrection day, our Lord gave His disciples the Holy Spirit to enable them to wait for the full outpouring on the day of Pentecost. It is only in the power of the Spirit already in us, acknowledged and yielded to, that we can pray for His fuller manifestation. Say to the Father, "It is the Spirit of your Son in me who is urging me to plead your promise."

SPECIAL PETITIONS

_____
_____
_____
_____
_____
_____
_____
_____

DAY THREE

What to Pray—for all saints

"Praying always with all prayer and supplication in the Spirit, and watching thereunto with all perseverance and supplication for all saints" (Eph. 6:18).

Every member of a body is interested in the welfare of the whole, and exists to help and complete the others. Believers are one body and ought to pray, not so much for the welfare of their own church or society, but, first of all, for all saints. This large, unselfish love is the proof that Christ's Spirit and love are teaching them to pray. Pray first for all believers and then for those around you.

How to Pray—in the love of the Spirit

"By this shall all men know that ye are my disciples, if ye have love one to another" (John 13:35).

"That they all may be one . . . that the world may believe that thou hast sent me" (John 17:21).

"I beseech you, brethren . . . for the love of the Spirit, that ye strive together with me in your prayers to God for me" (Rom. 15:30).

"Above all things have fervent charity among your selves" (1 Pet. 4:8).

If we are to pray we must love. Let us tell God we do love all His saints; let us say we love especially every child of His we know. Let us pray with fervent love, in the love of the Spirit.

SPECIAL PETITIONS

_____
_____
_____
_____
_____
_____
_____

DAY FOUR

What to Pray—for the Spirit of holiness

God is the Holy One. His people are a holy people. He speaks: "I am holy: I am the Lord which makes you holy." Christ prayed: "Sanctify them. Make them holy through thy truth." Paul prayed: "God establish your hearts unblameable in holiness." "God sanctify you wholly!"

Pray for all saints—God's holy ones—throughout the Church, that the Spirit of holiness may rule them. Especially pray for new converts. Pray for the saints in your own neighborhood or congregation. Pray for any you are especially interested in. Think of their special need, weakness or sin, and pray that God may make them holy.

How to Pray—trusting in God's omnipotence

The things that are impossible with men are possible with God. Think of the great things we ask for, of how little likelihood there is of their coming, of our own significance. Prayer is not only wishing, or asking, but believing and accepting. Be still before God and ask Him to allow you to know Him as the Almighty One, and leave your petitions with Him who does wonders.

SPECIAL PETITIONS

_____
_____
_____
_____
_____
_____
_____
_____

DAY FIVE

What to Pray—that God's people may be kept from the world

"Holy Father, keep through thine own name those whom thou hast given me. I pray not that thou shouldest take them out of the world, but that thou shouldest keep them from the evil. They are not of the world, even as I am not of the world" (John 17:11, 15, 16).

In the last night Christ asked three things for His disciples: that they might be kept as those who are not of the world; that they might be sanctified; that they might be one in love. You cannot do better than pray as Jesus prayed. Ask for God's people that they may be kept separate from the world and its spirit; that they, by the Holy Spirit, may live as those who are not of the world.

How to Pray—having confidence before God

"Beloved, if our heart condemn us not, then have we confidence toward God. And whatsoever we ask, we receive of him, because we keep his commandments, and do those things that are pleasing in his sight" (1 John 3:21, 22).

Learn these words by heart. Get them into your heart. Join the ranks of those who, with John, draw nigh to God with an assured heart, that does not condemn them, having confidence toward God. In this spirit pray for your brother who sins (1 John 5:16). In the quiet confidence of an obedient child, plead for those of your brethren who may be giving way to sin. Pray for all to be kept from the evil. And say often, "What we ask, we receive, because we keep and do."

SPECIAL PETITIONS

_____
_____
_____

DAY SIX

What to Pray—for the spirit of love in the church

"That they may be one, even as we are one: I in them and thou in me . . . that the world may know that thou hast sent me, and hast loved them, as thou hast loved me . . . that the love wherewith thou hast loved me may be in them, and I in them" (John 17:22, 23, 26).

"The fruit of the Spirit is love" (Gal. 5:22).

Believers are one in Christ, as He is one with the Father. The love of God rests on them, and can dwell in them. Pray that the power of the Holy Spirit may so work this love in believers that the world may see and know God's love in them. Pray much for this.

How to Pray—as one of God's reminders

"I have set watchmen upon thy walls . . . which shall never hold their peace day nor night: ye that make mention of the Lord, keep not silence, and give him no rest" (Isa. 62:6).

Study these words until your whole soul is filled with the consciousness: I am appointed intercessor. Enter God's presence in that faith. Study the world's need with this thought—it is my work to intercede; the Holy Spirit will teach me for what and how. Let it be an abiding consciousness: My great life work, like Christ's, is intercession—to pray for believers and those who do not yet know God.

SPECIAL PETITIONS

_____

_____

_____

_____

_____

_____

_____

_____

DAY SEVEN

What to Pray—for the power of the Holy Spirit on ministers

"I beseech you . . . that ye strive together with me in your prayers to God for me" (Rom. 15:30).

"He will yet deliver us; ye also helping together by prayer for us" (2 Cor. 1:10, 11).

What a great host of ministers there are in Christ's Church. What need they have of prayer. What a power they might be if they were all clothed with the power of the Holy Spirit. Pray definitely for this; long for it. Think of your own minister, and ask it very specially for him. Connect every thought of the ministry, in your town or neighborhood or the world, with the prayer that all may be filled with the Spirit. Plead for them the promise, "Tarry till ye be clothed with power from on high." "Ye shall receive power when the Holy Ghost is come upon you."

How to Pray—in secret

"But thou, when thou prayest, enter into thy closet, and when thou hast shut thy door, pray to the Father which is in secret" (Matt. 6:6).

"He departed again into the mountain himself alone" (Matt. 14:23; John 6:15).

Take time and realize, when you are alone with God: Here am I now, face to face with God, to intercede for His servants. Do not think you have no influence, or that your prayer will not be missed. Your prayer and faith will make a difference. Cry in secret to God for His ministers.

SPECIAL PETITIONS

_____
_____
_____
_____

DAY EIGHT

What to Pray—for the Spirit on all Christian workers

"Ye also helping together by prayer for us, that for the gift bestowed upon us by the means of many persons thanks may be given by many on our behalf" (2 Cor. 1:11).

What multitudes of workers in connection with our churches and missions, our railways and postmen, our soldiers and sailors, our young men and young women, our fallen men and women, our poor and sick. God be praised for this! What could they accomplish if each were living in the fullness of the Holy Spirit! Pray for them; it makes you a partner in their work, and you will praise God each time you hear of blessing anywhere.

How to Pray—with definite petitions

"What wilt thou that I shall do unto thee?" (Luke 18:41).

The Lord knew what the man wanted, and yet He asked him. The utterance of our wish gives point to the transaction in which we are engaged with God, and so awakens faith and expectation. Be very definite in your petitions so as to know what answer you may look for. Just think of the great host of workers, and ask and expect God definitely to bless them in answer to the prayers of His people. Then ask still more definitely for workers around you. Intercession is not the breathing out of pious wishes; its aim is, in believing, persevering prayer, to receive and bring down blessing.

SPECIAL PETITIONS

_____

_____

_____

_____

_____

DAY NINE

What to Pray—for God's Spirit
on our mission work

"As they ministered to the Lord, and fasted, the Holy Ghost said, Separate me Barnabas and Saul. . . . And when they had fasted and prayed . . . sent them away. So they, being sent forth by the Holy Ghost, departed" (Acts 13:2-4).

The evangelization of the world depends, first of all, upon a revival of prayer. Deeper than the need for men—deep down at the bottom of our spiritless life—is the need for the forgotten secret of prevailing, worldwide prayer.

Pray that our mission work may all be done in this spirit—waiting on God, hearing the voice of the Spirit, sending forth men with fasting and prayer. Pray that in our churches, our mission interest and mission work may be in the power of the Holy Spirit and of prayer. It is a Spirit-filled, praying church that will send out Spirit-filled missionaries, mighty in prayer.

How to Pray—take time

"I give myself unto prayer" (Ps. 109:4).
"We will give ourselves continually to prayer" (Acts 6:4).
"Be not rash with thy mouth, and let not thine heart be hasty to utter anything before God" (Eccles. 5:2).

Time is one of the chief standards of value. The time we give is a proof of the interest we feel.

We need time with God—to realize His presence; to wait for Him to make himself known; to consider and feel the needs we plead for; to take our place in Christ; to pray till we can believe that we have received. Take time in prayer and pray down blessing on the mission work of the Church.

SPECIAL PETITIONS

_____

_____
_____

134

DAY TEN

What to Pray—for God's Spirit on our missionaries

"Ye shall receive power, after that the Holy Ghost is come upon you: and ye shall be my witnesses unto. . . the uttermost part of the earth" (Acts 1:8).

What the world needs today is not only more missionaries, but also the outpouring of God's Spirit on everyone whom He has sent out to work for Him in the foreign field.

God always gives His servants power equal to the work He asks of them. Think of the greatness and difficulty of this work—casting out Satan from his strongholds—and pray that everyone who takes part in it may receive and do all his work in the power of the Holy Ghost. Think of the difficulties of your missionaries and pray for them.

How to Pray—trusting God's faithfulness

"He is faithful that promised. . . . She judged him faithful who had promised" (Heb. 10:23; 11:11).

Just think of God's promises to His Son concerning His kingdom; to the Church, concerning the heathen; to His servants, concerning their work; to yourself, concerning your prayer. Then pray in the assurance that He is faithful and only waits for prayer and faith to fulfill them. "Faithful is he that calleth you" (to pray), "who also will do it" (what He has promised).

Take up individual missionaries, make yourself one with them, and pray till you know that you are heard. Begin to live for Christ's kingdom as the one thing worth living for!

SPECIAL PETITIONS

_____

_____

_____

DAY ELEVEN

What to Pray—for more laborers

"Pray ye therefore the Lord of the harvest, that he will send forth labourers into his harvest" (Matt. 9:38).

What a remarkable call of the Lord Jesus for help from His disciples in getting the need supplied. What an honor put upon prayer. What a proof that God wants prayer and will hear it.

Pray for laborers, for all students in theological seminaries, training centers, Bible institutes, that they may not go unless He fits them and sends them forth; that our churches may train their students to seek for the sending forth of the Holy Spirit; that all believers may hold themselves ready to be sent forth or to pray for those who can go.

How to Pray—by faith, doubting nothing

"Jesus . . . saith unto them, Have faith in God. . . . Whosoever shall say unto this mountain, Be thou removed, and be thou cast into the sea; and shall not doubt in his heart, but shall believe that those things which he saith shall come to pass; he shall have whatsoever he saith" (Mark 11:22, 23).

Have faith in God! Ask Him to make himself known to you as the faithful, mighty God, who worketh all in all. You will be encouraged to believe that He can give suitable and sufficient laborers however impossible this appears—but, remember, in answer to prayer and faith.

Apply this to every opening where a good worker is needed. The work is God's. He can give the right workman. But He must be asked and waited upon.

SPECIAL PETITIONS

_____

_____

_____

_____

DAY TWELVE

What to Pray—for the Spirit to convince the world of sin

"I will send [the Comforter] unto you. And when he is come, he will reprove the world of sin" (John 16:7, 8).

God's one desire, the one object of Christ's being manifested, is to take away sin. The first work of the Spirit on the world is conviction of sin. Without that, no deep or abiding revival, no powerful conversion is possible. Pray for it, that the gospel may be preached in such power of the Spirit that men may see that they have rejected and crucified Christ and cry out, "What shall we do?"

Pray most earnestly for a mighty power of conviction of sin wherever the gospel is preached.

How to Pray—stir up yourself to take hold of God's strength

"Let him take hold of my strength, that he may make peace with me" (Isa. 27:5).

"There is none that calleth upon thy name, that stirreth up himself to take hold of thee" (Isa. 64:7).

"Stir up the gift of God, which is in thee" (2 Tim. 1:6).

First, take hold of God's strength. God is a Spirit. I cannot take hold of Him and hold Him fast but by the Spirit. Take hold of God's strength and hold on till it has done for you what He has promised. Pray for the power of the Spirit to convict of sin.

Second, by the power that is in you by the Holy Spirit stir up yourself to take hold. Give your whole heart and will to it and say, "I will not let Thee go except Thou bless me."

SPECIAL PETITIONS

_____
_____
_____
_____

DAY THIRTEEN

What to Pray—for the spirit of burning

"And it shall come to pass, that he that is left in Zion . . . shall be called holy. . . when the Lord shall have washed away the filth of the daughters of Zion . . . by the spirit of judgment and by the spirit of burning" (Isa. 4:3, 4).

A washing by fire! A cleansing by judgment! He that has passed through this shall be called holy. The power of blessing for the world, the power of work and intercession that will avail, depends upon the spiritual state of the Church. That state can only rise higher as sin is discovered and put away. Judgment must begin at the house of God. There must be conviction of sin for sanctification. Beseech God to give His Spirit as a spirit of judgment and a spirit of burning—to discover and burn out sin in His people.

How to Pray—in the name of Christ

"Whatsoever ye shall ask in my name, that will I do. . . . If ye shall ask anything in my name, that will I do" (John 14:13, 14).

Ask in the name of your Redeemer God who sits upon the throne. Ask what He has promised, what He gave His blood for, that sin may be put away from among His people. Ask—the prayer is after His own heart—for the spirit of deep conviction of sin to come among His people. Ask for the spirit of burning. Ask in the faith of His name—the faith of what He will and of what He can do—then look for the answer. Pray that the Church may be blessed, to be made a blessing in the world.

SPECIAL PETITIONS

_____
_____
_____
_____

138

DAY FOURTEEN

What to Pray—for the Church of the future

"[That the children] might not be as their fathers . . . a generation that set not their heart aright, and whose spirit was not steadfast with God" (Ps. 78:8).

"I will pour my spirit upon thy seed, and my blessing upon thine offspring" (Isa. 44:3).

Pray for the rising generation who are to come after us. Think of the young men and young women and children of this age and pray for all the agencies at work among them; that wherever they are, Christ may be honored and the Holy Spirit get possession of them. Pray for the young of your own neighborhood.

How to Pray—with the whole heart

"[The Lord] grant thee according to thine own heart" (Ps. 20:4).

"Thou hast given him his heart's desire" (Ps. 21:2).

"I cried with my whole heart; hear me, O Lord" (Ps. 119:145).

God lives and He listens to every petition with His whole heart. Each time we pray the whole infinite God is there to hear. He asks that in each prayer the whole man shall be there too; that we shall cry with our whole heart. Christ gave himself to God for men, and so He takes up every need into His intercession. If once we seek God with our whole heart, the whole heart will be in every prayer with which we come to this God. Pray with your whole heart for the young.

SPECIAL PETITIONS

_____
_____
_____
_____
_____
_____

What to Pray—for schools and colleges

"As for me, this is my covenant with them, saith the Lord; my Spirit that is upon thee, and my words which I have put in thy mouth, shall not depart out of thy month, nor out of the mouth of thy seed, nor out of the mouth of thy seed's seed, saith the Lord, from henceforth and for ever" (Isa. 59:21).

The future of the Church and the world depends—to an extent we little conceive—on the education of the day. The Church may be seeking to evangelize the heathen, and be giving up on her own children to secular and materialistic influences. Pray for schools and colleges, and that the Church may realize and fulfull its momentous duty of caring for its children. Pray for godly teachers.

How to Pray—not limiting God

"They . . . limited the Holy One of Israel" (Ps. 78:41).
"He did not many mighty works there because of their unbelief" (Matt. 13:58).
"Is anything too hard for the Lord?" (Gen. 18:14).
"Ah, Lord God! . . . thou hast made the heaven and the earth by thy great power . . . there is nothing too hard for thee. Behold, I am the Lord . . . is there anything too hard for me?" (Jer. 32:17, 27).

Above everything, beware in your prayer of limiting God, not only by unbelief, but by fancying that you know what He can do. Expect unexpected things, above all that we ask or think. Each time you intercede, be quiet first and worship God in His glory. Think of what He can do, of how He delights to hear Christ, of your place in Christ, and expect great things.

SPECIAL PETITIONS

_____

_____

_____

DAY SIXTEEN

What to Pray—for the power of the Holy Spirit in our Sunday schools

"Thus saith the Lord, Even the captives of the mighty shall be taken away, and the prey of the terrible shall be delivered; for I will contend with him that contendeth with thee, and I will save thy children" (Isa. 49:25).

Every part of the work of God's Church is His work. He must do it. Prayer is the confession that He will, the surrender of ourselves into His hands to let Him work in us and through us. Pray for hundreds of thousands of Sunday school teachers, that those who know God may be filled with His Spirit. Pray for your own Sunday school. Pray for the salvation of the children.

How to Pray—boldly

"We have a great High Priest . . . Jesus the Son of God. Let us therefore come boldly unto the throne of grace" (Heb. 4:14, 16).

These hints to help us in our work of intercession—what are they doing for us? Making us conscious of our feebleness in prayer? Thank God for this. It is the very first lesson we need on the way to pray the "effectual prayer that availeth much." Let us persevere, taking each subject boldly to the throne of grace. As we pray we shall learn to pray, and to believe, and to expect with increasing boldness. Hold fast your assurance; it is at God's command you come as an intercessor. Christ will give you grace to pray aright.

SPECIAL PETITIONS

_____

_____

_____

_____

_____

DAY SEVENTEEN

What to Pray—for kings and rulers

"I exhort therefore, that, first of all, supplications, prayers, intercessions, and giving of thanks, be made for all men; for kings, and for all that are in authority; that we may lead a quiet and peaceable life in all godliness and honesty" (1 Tim. 2:1, 2).

What a faith in the power of prayer! A few feeble and despised Christians are to influence the mighty Roman emperors and help in securing peace and quietness. Let us believe that prayer is a power that is taken up by God in His rule of the world. Let us pray for our country and its rulers, for all the rulers of the world, for rulers in cities or districts in which we are interested. When God's people unite in this, they may count upon their prayer affecting the unseen world more than they know. Let faith hold this fast.

How to Pray—the prayer before God as incense

"And another angel came and stood at the altar, having a golden censer; and there was given unto him much incense, that he should offer it with the prayers of all saints upon the golden altar which was before the throne. And the smoke of the incense, which came with the prayers of the saints, ascended up before God out of the angel's hand. And the angel took the censer, and filled it with fire of the altar, and cast it into the earth: and there were voices, and thunderings, and lightnings, and an earthquake" (Rev. 8:3-5).

The same censer brings the prayer of the saints before God and casts fire upon the earth. The prayers that go up to heaven have their share in the history of this earth. Be assured that your prayers enter God's presence.

SPECIAL PETITIONS

_____
_____
_____
_____
_____

DAY EIGHTEEN

What to Pray—for peace

"I exhort therefore that, first of all supplications . . . be made for . . . kings and for all that are in authority; that we may lead a quiet and peaceable life in all godliness and honesty. For this is good and acceptable in the sight of God our Saviour" (1 Tim. 2:1-3).

"He maketh wars to cease unto the end of the earth" (Ps. 46:9).

What a terrible sight—the military armaments in which the nations find their pride! What a terrible thought—the evil passions that may at any moment bring on war! And what a prospect the suffering and desolation that must come! God can, in answer to the prayer of His people, give peace. Let us pray for it and for the rule of righteousness on which alone it can be established.

How to Pray—with the understanding

"What is it then? I will pray with the spirit, and I will pray with the understanding" (1 Cor. 14:15).

We need to pray with the sprirt as the vehicle of the intercession of God's Spirit if we are to take hold of God in faith and power. We need to pray with the understanding if we are really to enter deeply into the needs we bring before Him. Take time to grasp intelligently in each subject, the nature, the extent, the urgency of the request, the ground and way and certainty of God's promise as revealed in His Word. Let the mind affect the heart. Pray with the understanding and with the spirit.

SPECIAL PETITIONS

_____

_____

_____

_____

_____

_____

DAY NINETEEN

What to Pray—for the Holy Spirit on Christendom

"Having a form of godliness, but denying the power thereof" (2 Tim. 3:5).

"Thou hast a name that thou livest and art dead" (Rev. 3:1).

There are hundreds of millions of nominal Christians. The state of the majority is unspeakably awful. Formality, worldliness, ungodliness, rejection of service for Christ, ignorance, and indifference—to what an extent does all this prevail? We pray for the heathen. Let us also pray for those bearing Christ's name, many in worse than heathen darkness.

Does not one feel as if one should begin to give up his life, and to cry day and night to God for souls? In answer to prayer God gives the power of the Holy Ghost.

How to Pray—in deep stillness of soul

"My soul waiteth upon God: from him cometh my salvation" (Ps. 62:1).

Prayer has its power in God alone. The nearer a man comes to God himself, the deeper he enters into God's will. The more he takes hold of God, the more power in prayer.

God must reveal himself. If it please Him to make himself known, He can make the heart conscious of His presence. Our posture must be that of holy reverence, of quiet waiting and adoration.

As your month of intercession passes on and you feel the greatness of your work, be still before God. Thus you will receive power to pray.

SPECIAL PETITIONS

_____

_____
_____

DAY TWENTY

What to Pray—for God's Spirit on the heathen

"Behold, these shall come from far: and, lo, these from . . . the land of Sinim" (Isa. 49:12).

"Princes shall come out of Egypt; Ethiopia shall soon stretch out her hands unto God" (Ps. 68:31).

"I the Lord will hasten it in his time" (Isa. 60:22).

Pray for the heathen who are yet without the word. Think of China, with her hundreds of millions without Christ. Think of dark Africa, with its millions. Think of millions a year going down into the thick darkness. If Christ gave His life for them, will you not do so? You can give yourself up to intercede for them.

If you have not yet begun, just begin with this simple monthly school of intercession. The ten minutes you give will make you feel this is not enough. God's Spirit will draw you on. Persevere, however weak you are. Ask God to give you some country or tribe to pray for. Can anything be nobler than to do as Christ did? Give your life for the heathen.

How to Pray—with confident expectation of an answer

"Call unto me, and I will answer thee, and shew thee great and mighty things, which thou knowest not" (Jer. 33:3).

"Thus saith the Lord God: I will yet for this be inquired of . . . to do it for them" (Ezek. 36:37).

Both texts refer to promises definitely made, but their fulfillment would depend upon prayer: God would be inquired of to do it.

Pray for God's fulfillment of His promises to His Son and His Church and expect the answer. Plead for the heathen. Plead God's promises.

SPECIAL PETITIONS

_____

_____

_____

DAY TWENTY-ONE

What to Pray—for God's Spirit on the Jews

"I will pour upon the house of David and upon the inhabitants of Jerusalem, the spirit of grace and of supplications, and they shall look upon me whom they have pierced" (Zech. 12:10).

"Brethren, my heart's desire and prayer to God for Israel is that they might be saved" (Rom. 10:1).

Pray for the Jews. Their return to the God of their fathers stands connected, in a way we cannot understand, with wonderful blessing to the Church and with the coming of our Lord Jesus. Let us not think that God has foreordained all this and that we cannot hasten it. In a divine and mysterious way God has connected His fulfillment of His promise with our prayer. His Spirit's intercession in us is God's forerunner of blessing. Pray for Israel and the work done among them. Pray too: "Amen. Even so, come, Lord Jesus"!

How to Pray—with the intercession of the Holy Spirit

"We know not what we should pray for as we ought; but the Spirit itself maketh intercession for us with groanings which cannot be uttered" (Rom. 8:26).

In your ignorance and feebleness believe in the secret indwelling and intercession of the Holy Spirit within you. Yield yourself to His life and leading habitually. He will help your infirmities in prayer. Plead the promises of God even where you do not see how they are to be fulfilled. God knows the mind of the Spirit, "because he maketh intercession for the saints according to the will of God." Pray with the simplicity of a little child; pray with the holy awe and reverence of one in whom God's Spirit dwells and prays.

SPECIAL PETITIONS

_____

_____

_____

DAY TWENTY-TWO

What to Pray—for all who are suffering

"Remember them that are in bonds, as bound with them; and them which suffer adversity as being yourselves in the body" (Heb. 13:3).

What a world of suffering we live in! How Jesus sacrificed all and identified himself with it! Let us in our measure do so too. The persecuted believers behind the Iron Curtain, the famine-stricken million sof Africa, the poverty and wretchedness of the Third World—and so much more; what suffering among those who know God and who know Him not. And then in smaller circles, in ten thousand homes and hearts, what sorrow! In our own neighborhood, how many needing help or comfort. Let us have a heart for and think of the suffering. It will stir us to pray, to work, to hope, to love more. And in a way and time we know not, God will hear our prayers.

How to Pray—praying always, and not fainting

"He spake a parable unto them to this end, that men ought always to pray, and not to faint" (Luke 18:1).

Do you not begin to feel prayer is really the help for this sinful world? What a need there is of unceasing prayer! The very greatness of the task makes us despair! What can our ten minutes of intercession avail? It is right we feel this: this is the way in which God is calling and preparing us to give our life to prayer. Give yourself wholly to God for men, and even in all your work, your heart will be poured out to men in love, and drawn up to God in dependence and expectation. To a heart thus led by the Holy Spirit, it is possible to pray always and not to faint.

SPECIAL PETITIONS

_____

_____

_____

_____

DAY TWENTY-THREE

What to Pray—for the Holy Spirit in your own work

"I also labour, striving according to his working, which worketh in me mightily" (Col. 1:29).

You have your own special work; make it a work of intercession. Paul labored, striving according to the working of God in him. Remember, God is not only the Creator, but the Great Workman who worketh all in all. You can do your work only in His strength by Him working in you through the Spirit. Intercede much for those among whom you work till God gives you life for them.

Let us all intercede too for each other, for every worker throughout God's Church, however solitary or unknown.

How to Pray—in God's very presence

"Draw nigh to God, and he will draw nigh to you" (James 4:8).

The nearness of God gives rest and power in prayer. The nearness of God is given to him who makes it his first object. "Draw nigh to God"; seek the nearness to Him, and He will give it; "He will draw nigh to you." Then it becomes easy to pray in faith.

Remember that when first God takes you into the school of intercession, it is almost more for your own sake than that of others. You have to be trained to love and wait and pray and believe. Only persevere. Learn to set yourself in His presence, to wait quietly for the assurance that He draws nigh. Enter His holy presence, wait there, and spread your work before Him. Intercede for the souls you are working among. Get a blessing from God, His Spirit into your own heart, for them.

SPECIAL PETITIONS

_____
_____
_____

DAY TWENTY-FOUR

What to Pray—for the Spirit on your own congregation

"Beginning at Jerusalem" (Luke 24:47).

Each one of us is connected with some congregation or circle of believers. They are to us the part of Christ's body with which we come into most direct contact. They have a special claim on our intercession. Let it be a settled matter between God and you that you are to labor in prayer on its behalf. Pray for the minister and all leaders or workers in it. Pray for the believers according to their needs. Pray for conversions. Pray for the power of the Spirit to manifest itself. Band yourself with others to join in secret in definite petitions. Let intercession be a definite work, carried on as systematically as preaching or Sunday school. And pray, expecting an answer.

How to Pray—continually

"Watchmen . . . which shall never hold their peace day nor night" (Isa. 62:6).
"His own elect, which cry day and night unto him" (Luke 18:7).
"Night and day praying exceedingly that we . . . might perfect that which is lacking in your faith" (1 Thess. 3:10).
"A widow indeed trusteth . . . in God, and continueth in supplications and prayers night and day" (1 Tim. 5:5).

When the glory of God, and the love of Christ, and the need of souls are revealed to us, the fire of this unceasing intercession will begin to burn in us for those who are near and those who are far off.

SPECIAL PETITIONS

DAY TWENTY-FIVE

What to Pray—for more conversions

"He is able to save them to the uttermost . . . seeing he ever liveth to make intercession" (Heb. 7:25).

"We will give ourselves continually to prayer and to the ministry of the word. . . . And the word of God increased; and the number of the disciples multiplied greatly" (Acts 6:4, 7).

Christ's power to save, and save completely, depends on His unceasing intercession. After the apostles withdrew themselves continually to prayer, the number of the disciples multiplied greatly.

As we in our day give ourselves to intercession, we shall have more and mightier conversions. Let us plead for this. Christ is exalted to give repentance. The Church exists with the divine purpose and promise of having conversions. Let us not be ashamed to confess our sin and feebleness, and cry to God for more conversions in Christian and heathen lands, and for those too whom you know and love. Plead for the salvation of sinners.

How to Pray—in deep humility

"Truth, Lord: yet the dogs eat of the crumbs. . . . O woman, great is thy faith: be it unto thee even as thou wilt" (Matt. 15:27, 28).

You feel unworthy and unable to pray aright. To accept this heartily, and to be content still to come and be blest in your unworthiness, is true humility. It proves its integrity by not seeking for anything, but simply trusting His grace. And so it is the very strength of a great faith, and gets a full answer. "Yet the dogs"— let that be your plea as you persevere for someone possibly possessed of the devil. Let not your littleness hinder you for a moment.

SPECIAL PETITIONS

DAY TWENTY-SIX

What to Pray—for the Holy Spirit on young converts

"[Peter and John] prayed for them, that they might receive the Holy Ghost (for as yet he was fallen upon none of them: only they were baptized into the name of the Lord Jesus)" (Acts 8:15, 16).

"Now he which stablisheth us with you in Christ, and hath anointed us, is God; who hath also . . . given the earnest of the Spirit in our hearts" (2 Cor. 1:21, 22).

Many new converts remain feeble; many fall into sin; many backslide entirely. If we pray for the Church, its growth in holiness and devotion to God's service, pray especially for the young converts. Many stand alone, surrounded by temptation; many have no teaching on the Spirit in them and the power of God to establish them; many are in heathen lands, surrounded by Satan's power. If you pray for the power of the Spirit in the Church, pray especially that every young convert may know that he may claim and receive the fullness of the Spirit.

How to Pray—without ceasing

"As for me, God forbid that I should sin against the Lord in ceasing to pray for you" (1 Sam. 12:23).

It is sin against the Lord to cease praying for others. When once we begin to see how absolutely indispensable intercession is, just as much a duty as loving God or believing in Christ, and how we are called and bound to it as believers, we shall feel that to cease intercession is grievous sin. Let us ask for grace to take up our place as priests with joy and give our life to bring down the blessing of heaven.

SPECIAL PETITIONS

_____

_____

_____

DAY TWENTY-SEVEN

What to Pray—that God's people may realize their calling

"I will bless thee . . . and thou shalt be a blessing: *in thee* shall *all families of the earth* be blessed" (Gen. 12:2, 3).

"God be merciful *unto us,* and bless *us;* and cause his face to shine *upon us.* That thy way may be known *upon earth,* thy saving health *among all nations*" (Ps. 67:1, 2).

Abraham was only blessed that he might be a blessing to all the earth. Israel prays for blessing that God may be known among all nations. Every believer, just as much as Abraham, is only blessed that he may carry God's blessing to the world.

Cry to God that His people may know this, that every believer is only to live for the interests of God and His kingdom. If this truth were preached and believed and practiced, what a revolution it would bring in our mission work. What a host of willing intercessors we should have. Plead with God to work it by the Holy Spirit.

How to Pray—as one who has accepted for himself what he asks for others

"The Holy Ghost fell on them, as on us at the beginning. . . . God gave them the like gift, as he did unto us" (Acts 11:15, 17).

As you pray for this great blessing on God's people, the Holy Spirit taking entire possession of them for God's service, yield yourself to God and claim the gift anew in faith. Let each thought of feebleness or shortcoming only make you the more urgent in prayer for others. As the blessing comes to them, you too will be helped. With every prayer for conversions or mission work, pray that God's people may know how wholly they belong to Him.

SPECIAL PETITIONS

What to Pray—that all God's people may know the Holy Spirit

"The Spirit of truth, whom the world cannot receive . . . but ye know him; for he dwelleth with you, and shall be in you" (John 14:17).
"Know ye not that your body is the temple of the Holy Ghost?" (1 Cor. 6:19).

The Holy Spirit is the power of God for the salvation of men. He only works as He dwells in the Church. He is given to enable believers to live wholly as God would have them live, in the full experience and witness of Him who saves completely.

Pray God that every one of His people know the Holy Spirit! That He, in all His fullness, is given to them! That they cannot expect to live as their Father would have without having Him in His fullness, without being filled with Him! Pray that all God's people, even away in churches gathered out of heathendom, may learn to say: "I believe in the Holy Ghost."

How to Pray—laboring fervently in prayer

"Epaphras, who is one of you . . . saluteth you, always labouring fervently for you in prayers, that ye may stand perfect and complete in all the will of God" (Col. 4:12).

To a healthy man labor is a delight; in what interests him he labors fervently. The believer who is in full health, whose heart is filled with God's Spirit, labors fervently in prayer. For what? That his brethren may stand perfect and complete in all the will of God; that they may know what God wills for them, how He calls them to live, and be led and walk by the Holy Ghost. Labor fervently in prayer that all God's children may know this is possible and sure.

SPECIAL PETITIONS

_____
_____
_____

DAY TWENTY-NINE

What to Pray—for the Spirit of intercession

"I have chosen you, and ordained you, that ye should go and bring forth fruit . . . that whatsoever ye shall ask of the Father in my name, he may give it you" (John 15:16).

"Hitherto ye have asked nothing in my name. . . . At that day ye shall ask in my name" (John 16:24, 26).

Has not our school of intercession taught us how little we have prayed in the name of Jesus? He promised His disciples: In that day, when the Holy Spirit comes upon you, ye shall ask in My name. Are there not tens of thousands with us who are mourning the lack of the power of intercession? Let our intercession today be for them and all God's children, that Christ may teach us that the Holy Spirit is in us; and what it is to live in His fullness, and to yield ourselves to His intercession work within us. The Church and the world need nothing so much as a mighty Spirit of intercession to bring down the power of God on earth. Pray for the descent from heaven of the Spirit of intercession for a great prayer revival.

How to Pray—abiding in Christ

"If ye abide in me, and my words abide in you, ye shall ask what ye will, and it shall be done unto you" (John 15:7).

Our acceptance with God, our access to Him, is all in Christ. As we consciously abide in Him we have the liberty—not a liberty to our old nature or our self-will, but the divine liberty from all self-will, to ask what we will in the power of the new nature, and it shall be done. Let us keep this place and believe even now that our intercession is heard, and that the Spirit of supplication will be given all around us.

SPECIAL PETITIONS

_____

_____

_____

DAY THIRTY

What to Pray—for the Holy Spirit with the Word of God

"Our gospel came not unto you in word only, but also in power, and in the Holy Ghost, and in much assurance" (1 Thess. 1:5).

"Them that have preached the gospel unto you with the Holy Ghost sent down from heaven" (1 Pet. 1:12).

Many Bibles are being circulated. Many sermons on the Bible are being preached. Many Bibles are being read in home and school. How little blessing when it comes "in word" only. What divine blessing and power when it comes "in the Holy Spirit," when it is preached "with the Holy Spirit sent forth from heaven." Pray for Bible circulation and preaching and teaching and reading, that it may all be in the Holy Spirit, with much prayer. Pray for the power of the Spirit with the word in your own neighborhood wherever it is being read or heard. Let every mention of "the Word of God" waken intercession.

How to Pray—watching and praying

"Continue in prayer, and watching in the same with thanksgiving; withal praying also for us that God would open unto us a door of utterance" (Col. 4:2, 3).

Do you not see how all depends upon God and prayer? As long as He lives and loves and hears and works, as long as there are souls with hearts closed to the Word, as long as there is work to be done in carrying the Word—pray without ceasing. "Continue in prayer, watching in the same with thanksgiving." These words are for every Christian.

SPECIAL PETITIONS

_____

_____

_____

What to Pray—for the Spirit of Christ in His people

"I am the vine, ye are the branches" (John 15:5).
"That ye should do as I have done to you" (John 13:15).

As branches we are to be so like the vine, so entirely identified with it, that all may see that we have the same nature and life and spirit. When we pray for the Spirit, let us not only think of a Spirit of power, but the very disposition and temper of Christ Jesus. Ask and expect nothing less. For yourself and all God's children, cry for it.

How to Pray—striving in prayer

"That ye strive together with me in your prayers to God for me" (Rom. 15:30).
"I would that ye knew what great conflict I have for you" (Col. 2:1).

All the powers of evil seek to hinder us in prayer. Prayer is a conflict with opposing forces. It needs the whole heart and all our strength. May God give us grace to strive in prayer till we prevail.

SPECIAL PETITIONS

_____
_____
_____
_____
_____
_____
_____
_____
_____
_____
_____